Sports Discourse

BLOOMSBURY DISCOURSE

Series Editor:
Professor Ken Hyland, University of Hong Kong

Discourse is one of the most significant concepts of contemporary thinking in the humanities and social sciences as it concerns the ways language mediates and shapes our interactions with each other and with the social, political and cultural formations of our society. The *Bloomsbury Discourse* aims to capture the fast-developing interest in discourse to provide students, new and experienced teachers and researchers in applied linguistics, ELT and English language with an essential bookshelf. Each book deals with a core topic in discourse studies to give an in-depth, structured and readable introduction to an aspect of the way language is used in real life.

Other titles in the series:

Academic Discourse, Ken Hyland
Corporate Discourse, Ruth Breeze
Discourse Analysis (2nd edition), Brian Paltridge
The Discourse of Blogs and Wikis, Greg Myers
The Discourse of Online Consumer Reviews, Camilla Vásquez
The Discourse of Text Messaging, Caroline Tagg
Discourse of Twitter and Social Media, Michele Zappavigna
Discourse Studies Reader, Edited by Ken Hyland
Historical Discourse, Caroline Coffin
Metadiscourse, Ken Hyland
News Discourse, Monika Bednarek and Helen Caple
Professional Discourse, Britt-Louise Gunnarsson
School Discourse, Frances Christie
Using Corpora in Discourse Analysis, Paul Baker
Workplace Discourse, Almut Koester

BLOOMSBURY DISCOURSE

Sports Discourse

TONY SCHIRATO

B L O O M S B U R Y

LONDON · NEW DELHI · NEW YORK · SYDNEY

Bloomsbury Academic

An imprint of Bloomsbury Publishing Plc

50 Bedford Square	1385 Broadway
London	New York
WC1B 3DP	NY 10018
UK	USA

www.bloomsbury.com

Bloomsbury is a registered trademark of Bloomsbury Publishing Plc

First published 2013

© Tony Schirato, 2013

British Library Cataloguing-in-Publication Data
A catalogue record for this book is available from the British Library.

ISBN: HB: 978-1-4411-1919-3
ePub: 978-1-4411-1586-7
ePDF: 978-1-4411-7336-2

Library of Congress Cataloging-in-Publication Data
A catalog record for this book is available from the Library of Congress.

Design by Newgen Knowledge Works (P) Ltd., Chennai, India
Printed and bound in India

CONTENTS

CHAPTER ONE

Discourse and critical theory

Introduction

This book aims to give an account of the cultural field of sport by way of a consideration of the discourses (both historical and contemporary) that are specific to, and play a significant role within and across, that field. We can justify this approach – specifically this emphasis on discursive practices and regimes – by invoking Michel Foucault's statement that discourses are not just a collection of signs, but 'practices that systematically form the objects of which they speak' (Foucault 1972: 49). What this means is that the events, sites, contests, organizations, rules, infrastructure, technologies and bodies that constitute the context, materiality and the visual and emotional realities of sport, from an impromptu kick-about in a backstreet to the media-intensive coverage of a World Cup or Olympic final, are experienced and rendered explicable and meaningful by way of the discursive frames applied to them. We can elaborate by considering what exactly is at stake in Foucault's statement on discourse. For John Frow:

> Each element of this sentence matters: discourses are practices in the sense that they carry out an action; they are systematic because they are relatively coherent in the way they work; they are formative of objects in the very act of speaking of them, not in the sense that they create objects out of nothing but in so far as they build a weight of meaning around the categories of the world. Discourses . . . are performative structures that shape the world in the very process of putting it into speech. (2006: 17–18)

Discourses are not simply a reflection of something that is already there, or a representation of existing meaning and form; rather they determine how we experience, order and evaluate the world. They are able to perform their work because they are seemingly consistent and continuous (although subject to historical and contextual change and variations) in terms of both their internal logics and relations, and their forms of addressing and interacting with subjects; so, for example, watching a game of football, either live or through the media, is to be involved in a communicative practice that presumes certain discursive categories of identity (fan, player, spectator), as well as performatives associated with those categories. These categories never appear or accrue meaning naturally; rather, they are produced and maintained, and acquire meaning, through the workings and movements of power. As Nietzsche (1974) points out, these changes can be read as the traces of power's historical trajectories across fields, societies and cultures.

The discourses and practices of a cultural field are constituted by and through relations of power, which produce the categories, forms and mechanisms that subjects use to understand and negotiate the world. As Pierre Bourdieu writes:

> I, as a thing for which there are things, comprehend this world. And I do so . . . because it encompasses me and comprehends me, it is through this material inclusion – often unnoticed and repressed – and what follows from it, the incorporation of social structures in the form of dispositional structures . . . that I acquire a practical knowledge and control of the encompassing space. (2000: 130)

Discourse acts as a facility, a medium and a technical apparatus that enables the perception, categorization, differentiation and explication of the world. We live within and experience a world which is given to us by and through discourses; and subjects are necessarily shaped, constrained and disposed towards thoughts and actions through their immersion in, and their incorporation of, the discourses of a cultural field (such as school, the family and most particularly the media).

In this chapter, we will provide an account of and demonstrate the ways in which discourse does its work – that is, functions as a practical, systematic and performative structure that produces the world-as-meaning. We will begin by looking in detail some relevant theoretical issues and accounts relevant to discourse and social practice. We will deal with language games and communication, and theories of the relation between discursive regimes, cultural fields and subjectivity.

Language games

Ludwig Wittgenstein proposed that language can be understood as a form of work, or a 'set of instruments for particular uses' (Wittgenstein 1983:

99); and that representations and accounts of the world are constituted from and arranged in terms of a systematic logic, what he calls 'a distribution in space' (187) that is not natural or immanent to the world. For Wittgenstein, all language systems – visual, verbal and scriptural – are not connected by any one set of formal properties (shared forms of grammar, for instance); rather, they are cognate in terms of their relation to the things they produce and manifest. Wittgenstein explains this by describing language as a game, not in the sense that it is playful, trivial or non-serious, but because like any game it is made up of systematic rules that practitioners commit to and follow. Take the example of two workers who devise a game based on throwing a ball against an office wall and catching it. The rules will complement their circumstances and context, which would include the dimensions of the playing space, the time allocated, the consistency and materiality of the ball, and the contours and dimensions of the wall. The basic rules – the ball must be propelled with an upward motion, land above a point on the wall, be caught before it hits the ground and land within a designated area (corresponding to a section of the office carpet) – produce effects in the form of bodily movements and trajectories, tactics and strategies, and affective experiences (tied in with the results and performances). Above all else, however, it produces a specific form of 'between us' on the part of the players, in the sense that every move in the game constitutes an expression of the rules which must elicit a response or reciprocity if the game is to continue. In short, the players' movements, thoughts and feelings in time and space are derived from and commensurate with regard to the architecture of the game.

For Wittgenstein all the things of language are basically an 'expression of a rule in a language game' (1983: 26), and his work attempts to show how this relation is fundamental to and inflects all communicative practices, and to 'bring words back from their metaphysical to their everyday use' (48). He identifies and deals with four issues that are germane to this project. First, he argues that the disjunction between language and the world they claim to deliver up is erased or covered over through techniques of reception, such as reading, listening, hearing, seeing, identifying, categorizing, analysing and interpreting. As Wittgenstein observes by way of example 'we do not find the whole business of seeing puzzling enough . . . If you look at a photograph of people, houses and trees, you do not feel the lack of the third dimension in it' (213). Second, when we read, analyse and interpret communication acts and discourse practices, there is a tendency to presume that we are talking about, arguing over and dealing with the status, characteristics, meaning or value of things, when in fact the objects of interpretation are also the mediums of interpretation, not the world itself. As Wittgenstein writes 'One thinks one is tracing the outline of the things of nature . . . when one is merely tracing round the frame through which we look at it' (48). Third, and by way of extension, giving an account of or reporting about something is a practice which, rather than telling us about that thing, informs us 'about the person making the report' (190). What a person says to another person, say in a romantic situation, may not be true, accurate or remotely reliable ('I promise to love you forever', 'My partner doesn't understand me'), but it does allow us to analyse, identify, categorize and evaluate what the speaker is doing, and how they are trying to produce a particular social form of 'between us'. Fourth and finally, making sense of texts (including visual texts) is both a form of work and the product of a regime of training; what is seen, the meanings that are identified or made, and the evaluation of the text is predicated on the wider cultural trajectories, dispositions and literacies of subjects. Every text signals to the reader, usually in a manner commensurate with the relevant genre (obvious with children's literature or a training manual, more subtle in scientific, literary or scholarly works), and utilizes conventional signposting to inflect or guide the reader's train of thought. For Wittgenstein, reading and interpretation can be defined as 'the relation between training and reacting' (80).

Discourse and cultural fields

Everything we have considered with regard to the relation between language-as-discourse and everyday thoughts and practices applies both to sport as a cultural field, and to the experiences of the members (sportspeople, administrators, fans, spectators) of that field. A cultural field is an imagined community in Ben Anderson's (1991) sense of the term; it is consequent of a successful act of discursive articulation that disposes subjects and institutions to identify with the name and the concept of sport. The values associated with this concept produce the 'between us' that facilitates communal identification: they constitute the glue that binds the community together.

It was the production, articulation, dissemination and acceptance of certain orders of discourse, ones that emphasized fair play, *askesis*, competition, team work, amateurism, the benefits and pleasures of play, rationality, uniformity and standardization, that 'systematically formed the object of which they spoke', and brought the cultural field of sport into being in the mid-nineteenth century. This did not mean that there was a necessary articulation or congruence between the practices, identities and discourses of sport; or that the field and its practices and practitioners were all committed to, believed in, and acted in accordance with, dominant beliefs, rules and values. However those discourses, and their norms and prescriptions, came to constitute the standard against which practices and performances could and would be judged; and in the process they determined who was to be included in or excluded from the field. Cavalry officers, for instance, could compete in early Olympic equestrian events because it was assumed that they did not acquire their skills for monetary gain; their subordinates, on the other hand, were tainted, and disqualified from competing, because of their need to work and earn a living.

Sports discourse also constituted the basis on which members of the field came to see and understand their relation to the field and the wider socio-cultural sphere: they worked to naturalize and universalize a particular world-view and set of attitudes, produced bodily forms and praxis, and disposed subjects with regard to their desires, pleasures, tastes, interests and aspirations. The masculinist character of sports discourse, for instance, completely orients and disposes a reading of the athletic body. The sight of male athletes staggering or collapsing while finishing a race effectively reinscribes and naturalizes the link between competitiveness, endurance, resilience and self-overcoming, and masculinity; in other words, a semiotics of distress, pain, suffering and discomfort is what is expected of, and commensurate with, the male athlete. The same physical symptoms, situated on the female body, have functioned to disqualify women as part of sport (or at least physically taxing sports).

Capitalized ideas

We can demonstrate how this regulatory process works by way of reference to what Claude Lefort calls 'capitalized ideas', a theoretical position commensurate with Foucault's notion of the regulatory function of discursive regimes. John Thompson writes that for Lefort, in the nineteenth century:

> bourgeois ideology gradually broke its links with religious discourse and discarded the reference to a spiritual or physical elsewhere. In place of this elsewhere it substituted general, abstract ideas; the text of bourgeois ideology . . . is written in capital letters: Humanity, Progress, Science, Property, Family, Nation. These ideas are both representative and rules, in the sense that they imply a certain way of acting which is consistent with the idea. The ideas thus give rise to an opposition between the subject who speaks and acts in accordance with the rule, and the 'other' who has no access to the rule and is therefore deprived of the status of subject. (1986: 17)

The regulation of social practice through the appropriation and deployment of these capitalized ideas is one obvious way of loading the dice of cultural politics because it acts to literally exclude certain groups (woman, children, non-whites) from the game itself (by designating them as less than full subjects). Capitalized ideas are deployed as signs that authorize an argument, position, categorization, policy or course of action. The term 'sportsmanship', for instance, constitutes one of the most significant of the many capitalized ideas that characterize the field of sport. It is also, for that reason, one of the most difficult terms to challenge, to engage with, or even to bring to discussion and analysis. It does its work quickly and without fuss, precisely because any questioning of what the terms mean, how it is being used, and for what purposes, is effectively foreclosed. In this way it largely resists critical inquiry.

It is not correct to say that capitalized ideas are empty of content; rather we can characterize the status of the content associated with them as arbitrary, but motivated. 'Sportsmanship' has no natural content of its own; rather it is filled in by and becomes associated with the discourses, narratives, stories, examples and meanings of truth, produced by and through networks of practices of power. The content is arbitrary in the sense that it can be changed, transformed, edited and replaced at a particular historical time and place. It is motivated because the meanings, narratives and exemplifications are oriented towards performing a certain discursive work; for instance, the association of some thing (a group, an action, an attitude, a form of bodily hexis) with natural meaning and value.

Discursive regimes

The site where this relation between training and reacting, and by extension the production and negotiation of meaning, is most intensively played out is at the level of discourse. In *The Archaeology of Knowledge*, Foucault refers to discourse as the 'What was being said in what was being said' (1972: 28); by which he means, among other things, that it constitutes the rules that bring about the emergence of, and order and make meaningful, the things of language. For Foucault, discourse is language that manifests itself as a specific architectural form, and which has been assigned certain tasks and forms of work. One of the tasks that discourse analysis takes on, from this perspective, is to demonstrate that discourse is not:

> a slender surface of contact, or confrontation, between a reality and a language, the interaction of a lexicon and an experience . . . in analysing discourses themselves, one sees the loosening of the embrace, apparently so tight, of words and things, and the emergence of a group of rules proper to discursive practice. These rules define not the dumb existence of a reality . . . but the ordering of objects. Of course, discourses are composed of signs; but what they do is more than use these signs to designate things. It is this more that renders them irreducible to . . . language and speech. It is this more that we must reveal and describe. (48–9)

In order to explain and demonstrate the relationship between discourse as an organizing principle and a set of communication practices, Foucault makes uses of the concepts of the 'discursive regime' (or 'formation') and 'discursive event', which he more commonly refers to as a 'statement'; by way of analogy, he suggests that 'A statement belongs to a discursive formation as a sentence belongs to a text' (1972: 116). Statements need not be sentences or linguistic utterances in any conventional sense: Foucault (1972) refers to the arrangement of keys on a typewriter, and graphs and other statistical devices, as statements. With regard to the field of sport, we could say that the records of the fixture lists of English County Cricket could be read as a history of statements that reflected significant changes to the discursive regime of sport from the mid-nineteenth to the twenty-first century. Until 1890, fixtures had been arranged in a more or less arbitrary (although motivated and traditional) manner, and there was no consistency with regard to the number of games played or the range or quality of opponents. The question of who could claim to be champions had to be considered retrospectively, and by various non-official means (in the newspapers, by general acclamation, by a club referring to itself as champions without being challenged), because the fixture list was not oriented towards producing results that could form the basis for, or were commensurate with, determining a champion team. The fixture lists of the period from the eighteenth to the late nineteenth century gradually (but inconsistently) took on and exhibited the characteristics (bureaucratization, standardization, continuity, consistency, quantification) of what Allan Guttmann (1978) has called the modernization of sport. At the same time they indicate that, contrary to the contemporary situation, the field of sport was slow to embrace the notion that winning, or determining an ultimate winner, was a paramount concern. However, in 1890, fixtures were reorganized so as produce official champions; and by the end of the twentieth century they had taken on an even more complex form of arrangement, one that emphasized economic considerations, most particularly the need to sell the game to and accommodate the interests of spectators and the media.

These reorganizations of fixture lists functioned as discursive statements; changes to the rules of play, the composition of the championship, the collection and availability of certain forms of statistical information, and the logic used to allocate points could also be singled out as examples. They were tied to, and derived from, significant movements that occurred within the discursive regime of the field of sport. Discursive regimes systematically regulate the production, organization and deployment of statements; and when a statement appears its particularity (this statement, rather than another) is at the same time an extrapolation from and a practice commensurate with regard to the rules of the discursive regime. The history of the choice and deployment of one statement over other possibilities, and the identification of the 'systems of dispersal' (Foucault 1972: 37) that govern these activities, is the primary focus of the study of discursive regimes. For Foucault, this analysis of discursive regimes needs to consider and address two complex methodological issues. First, it has to demonstrate their relation to everyday life; in other words, to show how discursive regimes (and their statements, logics and imperatives) produce, naturalize and maintain a world-view and a set of practices. Second, it needs to incorporate an explanation as to why statements appear at certain times and places, what legitimates them, and what accounts for their success or failure.

Genealogy

Foucault utilizes the Nietzschean concept of genealogy to help explain the processes and logics whereby discourses and statements are produced, activated and dispersed within and across fields, and over wider historical periods; and by extension how beliefs, rules and dispositions are embodied and maintained at the level of the everyday. What constitutes 'sportsmanship', for instance, is open to genealogical inquiry: we could trace it back to its points of origin, and identify the various inflection, changes and forms of emphasis that the term underwent during the nineteenth and twentieth centuries, and analyse the circumstances, contexts and forces that produced them. It is interesting to consider how, when and why, for instance, the sport of cricket became synonymous with sportsmanship, and how this imbrication took on various forms of socio-cultural work. Keith Sandiford (1994) refers to the Rev. Thomas Waugh book *The Cricket Field of a Christian Life* as an example of how:

> Cricket, morality and religion had become intermixed in the Victorian ethos. In Waugh's book . . . the Christian team is batting against Satan's devious and immoral bowlers who blatantly disregard the rules of the game. The godly batsman must therefore cope not only with the quality of the bowling itself but also with the attitude of the ungodly bowlers. It is significant, in analysing the late-Victorian frame of mind, to notice that Waugh chose to write about cricket rather than soccer and that his Christians were batsman and not bowlers. He adopted, in other words, the Victorian habit of glorifying the bat at the expense of the ball, while also supporting the popular view that soccer led to too many emotional excesses. (36)

Sandiford's point is that batting and cricket had strong discursive affiliations with the upper class, while bowing and soccer were considered more suitable and appropriate to the lower classes; this example parallels Nietzsche's observation that the genealogy of the notion of 'nobility' brings to light a process whereby a particular class group (the aristocracy) managed to make themselves synonymous with cultural value; in other words the circulation of the idea of noble character and behaviour as a natural category simultaneously transferred value back to the particular class to which the term was associated (Nietzsche 1956).

The study of sports discourse is, on one level, a study of how the field comes to know, understand and articulate itself, since every change in the discursive practices of the field serves as a kind of archaeological record (in Foucault's sense) of the historical interactions and relationships both within the field and between sport and other important fields (business, media, government, education). The field of sport was, from its inception, inflected by other fields and their values, logics, imperatives, forms of capital, technologies, identities and discourses. If we want to know where the field of sport has come from, where it is going to, and why, then we need to be able to identify and analyse those moments, sites, occasion and events when the field and its practitioners have, collectively and yet more or less unconsciously, become something else, something that the field of sport in its earlier incarnations might not recognize. Genealogy provides an account and explanation of this process, demonstrating how power relations, categories, meanings and discourses are produced, activated and dispersed within and across cultural fields, and maintained or transformed over time.

Foucault insists the body is central to genealogy, because it is the site both to which power is directed, and where it manifests itself. In a discussion of the methodological practice of genealogy, Foucault (1986a) refers to the process whereby a particular idea of truth, a belief system, or even a scientific methodology emerges and attaches itself to the body:

> It inscribes itself in the nervous system . . . The body manifests the stigmata of past experience and also gives rise to desires, failings, and errors . . . The body is the inscribed surface of events . . . Genealogy, as an analysis of descent, is thus situated within the articulation of the body and history. Its task is to expose a body totally imprinted by history and the process of history's destruction of the body. (148)

It is possible to observe how in everyday situations bodies perform, naturally and intuitively, their gender category, their class position and their place within a cultural field (familiar/stranger, important/insignificant, culturally literate/illiterate). In a television series such as Downton Abbey, for instance, the lower-class bodies seamlessly enact their deferment or subordination to members of a higher class (servants with their masters, craftspeople with wealthy clients), while the upper class perform their superiority through an ease of movement and a bodily semiotics of relaxation, disinterestedness and, by extension, control (Bourdieu 1991). This manifestation of bodily difference and distinction as a form of class politics was played out in FA cup ties in the 1880s, which frequently matched amateur teams made up of ex-public schoolboys with northern working-class teams. In the cup final of 1883 the eventual winners Blackburn Olympic was comprised of weavers, iron workers, clerks and a publican who arrived in London well before the game, trained long and hard and observed a strict diet, while their opponents the Old Etonians rolled up:

> [A]t the last moment . . . Who needs training when you have the future Lord High Commissioner for the Church of Scotland, a dilettante gentleman farmer, a Professor of Latin, the leading commercial lawyer in British India and a baronet by the name of Percy de Paravicini? (Goldblatt 2007: 43)

Discourse, subjectivity and performativity

For Foucault the subject as body only emerges by way of the workings of the discourses, categories and procedures of power: 'juridical systems of power produce the subjects they subsequently come to represent' (Butler 1990: 2). This means that all forms of subjectivity and identity are based on and linked to social and legal procedures, processes, techniques, norms and structures. In order to have, gain, claim or be assigned an identity, a person must be recognizable and explicable within a grid of intelligibility that both makes the subject appear, and authorizes that subject's status as an identity-in-waiting. The production of subjectivity is effected when the subject's body and behaviour is accepted as being commensurate with relevant socio-cultural or scientific discursive categories. To appear as a subject and to be granted an identity is thus to be inscribed in terms of certain meanings, values, dispositions, orientations and narratives, understood as normative categories.

Discourses and systems of categorization both naturalize a certain mediated version of the world, and simultaneously render anything else more or less unthinkable. Subjects are only identifiable as human because – at a certain time, in a certain place, for certain institutions – they are characterized by markers and performances that have been assimilated into, and institutionalized as, authorized cultural categories (at the level of gender, age, class, profession, race and ethnicity). Judith Butler argues (1900, 1993, 1997) that the relation between cultural performances and cultural fields (and the forms of subjectivity and identity they produce) is effectively a circular process: cultural fields, institutions, techniques and mechanisms produce subjects who are inclined to see and understand the world in terms of recognizable and authorized categories and their commensurate performances. This produces iterations of compliant performances, in turn accentuating and legitimizing those original templates. These dispositions are manifested as technically explicable practices, and reinforced and complemented by authorized, iterative performances of normal subjectivity (Butler 1993). This evaluation and categorization of each and every subject, including the self, is 'neither a single act nor a causal process initiated by the subject . . . Construction not only takes place in time, but is itself a temporal process which operates through the reiteration of norms' (10). Butler points out, however, that this process is both reproductive and potentially dynamic. There are sites and times in a culture where performances of subjectivity come to embody and play out the tensions, ambiguities and changes to what is understood as acceptable and normal both within a specific cultural field, and more generally across the social field and the field of power. We can monitor whether our subjectivity is 'on track' in terms of our body shape, clothes, mannerisms, or ways of seeing and evaluating other people. These images, ideas and performances constitute a vast store of up-to-date templates for, or models of, a normal, healthy, attractive and desirable subject. This evaluation and categorization of each and every subject, including the self, is 'neither a single act nor a causal process initiated by the subject . . . Construction not only takes place in time, but is itself a temporal process which operates through the reiteration of norms' (10).

The efficacy of this process can be observed in the way sportspersons' bodies perform, naturally and intuitively, the field and their place within the field. The body moves fluidly and naturally with regard to the tempos, rhythms and physical demands of the contest: an ice hockey player skates to where the puck is going before the teammate makes or sees the possibility of the pass; a goalie intuitively calculates when to move out to dispossess an advancing forward, and when to stay back and wait for a defender to intervene. The sporting body also manifests the values and principles of the field: it is honed, supple and flexible, strong, muscular but graceful, and prepared for and capable of enduring stress, hardship and physical punishment without wilting or faltering. It carries the field with(in) it, and consequently is able to negotiate the world in terms of what Bourdieu refers to as the facility of *illusio*, understood as literacy and confidence that is derived from the successful incorporation of the logics and forms of knowledge of the field (Bourdieu 2000). As Bourdieu writes:

> The world is comprehensible, immediately endowed with meaning, because the body, which, thanks to its senses and its brain, has the capacity to be present to what is outside itself, in the world, and to be impressed and durably modified by it, has been protractedly (from the beginning) exposed to its regularities. Having acquired from this exposure a system of dispositions attuned to these regularities, it is inclined and able to anticipate them practically in behaviours which engage a corporeal knowledge that provides a practical comprehension of the world quite different from the intentional acts of conscious decoding that is normally designated by the idea of comprehension. (135)

Much as we have done with County Cricket fixture lists, we could say that the players' bodies, and more generally their bodily hexis (which can be understood as the relation between social dispositions and the way the body is organized, arranged, deployed and presented) constitute discursive statements. If we take the celebrations of footballers who have scored a goal in contemporary professional football as a series of texts, and compared them with the reactions and responses of goal scorers in games in the first half of the twentieth century, we could extrapolate from these examples and make certain judgements about how they reflect or manifest changes to the field of sport over that period. For instance, from the 1930s to the present there has been a marked intensification in the celebration of goal scoring. In film of the 1930 and 1934 World Cup Finals we see that celebrations are instantaneous but relatively restrained by modern standards: usually players embrace, but some times the goal scorer will simply get a congratulatory pat on the back; and much the same is true of the dramatic 1954 final involving West Germany and Hungary. In the 1966 World Cup Final, the players are much more performative and active in their celebrations; they run away from the scene with their arms wide out, or jump, gesticulate and gesture demonstratively. When Andres Iniesta scores the winning goal in the 2010 final, however, things are of an altogether different (discursive) order. He pulls his shirt over his head, runs wildly to the sideline and is buried under players, reserves, trainers and coaches; he is not so much a player interacting with teammates as, in Guy Debord's (2006) terms, a form of media spectacle.

There is also a marked difference in the orientation of the celebrations, and the interaction of the players. In the older examples the players don't move very far from the scene of the goal before they are surrounded by teammates: in such cases, movement is spontaneous and lively. In the 2010 World Cup Final there is more drama apparent in the bodily hexis of players who missed chances (hands to heads, bodies slumping to the ground, looks of despair and anguish, screaming) than goal scorers in earlier games. Moreover in the 2010 final, Iniesta doesn't wait for others to congratulate him, or even run towards them; instead, he runs away from his teammates towards the coaches, reserves and groups of spectators. This is a common but relatively recent development in contemporary football: in the act of celebrating the player is distanced from (and often evades or pushes off) teammates. Even in those situations where the non-scoring player had done all the work, beating opponents and leaving the scorer to tap the ball into the empty net, it is not uncommon for the scorer to ignore the player who set him on and run towards the cameras. This development – the scorer running from teammates, but engaging with coaches, spectators and the media, or taking all the attention upon him or herself – would have been unthinkable before the Second World War, and probably was still a rarity in the 1970s.

One interpretation would be that this shows that contemporary players are more selfish and less team oriented; or again that there is greater pressure (emanating from the media, fans, financial considerations) which changes celebrations from expressions of joy to intense relief (which is why victory in major events is often occasioned by players weeping uncontrollably). To some extent these readings are valid, but they ignore equally if not more important considerations, such as the point that the incorporation of football into the wider field of entertainment, and the strong influenced exerted by the logics and imperatives of the media, means that celebrations are now more or less required to be attention grabbing, strongly affective and dramatic, because by and large the game sells itself (to fans, the media, business) as a passionate activity. Celebrations are now part of the spectacle of sport; in adding to the hyperbole, they help commoditize the game, the players involved (who sometimes become best known, not for their ability, but for the intricacy or eccentricity of the dance, gesture or bodily pose that accompanies scoring), and more widely, the cultural field of sport.

Cultural fields and the habitus

A cultural field can be said to have come into being when it fulfils at least three criteria. First, it must be able to articulate and manifest itself, simultaneously, as a singularity and a differentiated but cognate group of entities joined together by, and recognizable in terms of, certain core discourses, imperatives, values, functions, rules, categories and practices. Second, it must be recognized and accepted by, integrated into, and function in compliance with regard to, the network of fields that comprise the field of power (Bourdieu 1998b). Third, it must be able to demonstrate that its own ethos is commensurate with, and its work contributes to, the values and well-being of the wider socio-cultural field. In order for this to happen, a field must have the means and techniques to imagine itself into existence, and then to articulate, represent, manifest and valorize itself in a consistent manner to its own members and to other fields.

The viability of sport as a cultural field is necessarily predicated, then, on some degree of bureaucratization of people, activities and events within a regime that is specific and universal, changeable and timeless, and above all else able to reproduce itself across its members. The process whereby discursive formations naturalize themselves with regard to, and impose themselves upon, the subjects of a field is carried out via the epistemological mechanism of the habitus, which Bourdieu, Dauncey and Hare define as:

> generative principles of distinct and distinctive practices . . . habitus are also classificatory schemes, principles of classification, principles of vision and division, different tastes. They make distinctions between what is good and what is bad, between what is right and what is wrong, between what is distinguished and what is vulgar . . . But the essential point is that, when perceived through these social categories of perception . . . constitute a veritable language. (1998: 8)

It is not unreasonable to suggest that by the end of the nineteenth century the status, popularity and institutionalized nature of activities such as cricket, football, rugby and rowing testified to the transformation of a more or less random collection of games and physical activities into a recognizable and relatively autonomous cultural field, with a concomitant set of values, logics and dispositions, animated by and reproduced through a distinctive habitus. This was manifested in various ways, such as the spread and influence of the idea of the superiority of participating in games rather than simply winning them; the production of the body as a critical site of pedagogy and discipline; new forms of pleasure-as-spectatorship; the forging of a sense of communal identity through an association with sporting teams and, perhaps most significantly, the development of an entirely new relationship to the notion of play. The field and habitus of sport colonized Victorian society and culture completely, with the exception of a small number of cultural critics such as Mathew Arnold and Kipling; and it did so to the extent that its discourse were eventually interchangeable with pronouncements about English or British national character.

Cultural fields are simultaneously constituted through, and constitutive of, the habitus; its ethos and set of dispositions are embodied by its members, animate and justify its practices, and speak (through and for) the field as a discourse-of-belief. The sporting habitus gradually became to be seen and accepted by the Victorian socio-cultural field as more or less commensurate with Englishness, via a process which never forced itself upon or was importunate with regard to other fields or demographics. One of the secrets of the success of public school athletics, for instance, was that it presented itself as a series of values, dispositions and bodily practices that came naturally to the subject at the level of the body. As Bourdieu writes:

> There is every reason to think that the factors which are most influential in the formation of the habitus are transmitted without passing through . . . consciousness, but through suggestions inscribed in the most apparently insignificant aspects of the things, situations and practices of everyday life. Thus the modalities of practices, the ways of looking, sitting, standing, keeping silent or even of speaking . . . are full of injunctions that are powerful and hard to resist precisely because they are silent and insidious, insistent and insinuating. (2005: 51)

While the habitus is marked by its durability, every cultural field is inflected, to some extent, by both the field of power and those factors and contexts that are felt across the wider social field. This requires improvisations within the field, which taken cumulatively gradually produce different ways of seeing and experiencing the same types of activities. The habitus has the capacity to maintain itself, and continue to be productive, sometimes even in contexts where its orientation is contrary to self-interest. In such situations (when a subject moves into a new, and discursively antithetical field; or the field has been transformed) the habitus either moves seamlessly across to accommodate the new set of discursive conditions, or it remains left behind and 'out of time'.

Sport constitutes such an example: at a discursive level football-as-sport specifically and unambiguously elevates, values and commits to principles (such as fair play) that are irreducible to the logics of capitalism and the media, even after the transformation of football into a form of media-as-business. Two closely related examples of the playing out of this contradiction occurred in English football in the 2000–1 season. In the first instance, an FA cup tie between Arsenal and Sheffield United, an Arsenal player was injured, and a Sheffield United player kicked the ball out to stop the game until he recovered. When the game resumed an Arsenal player threw the ball back to the opposition, but another Arsenal player intercepted it and crossed to a teammate, who had 'no choice' but to score – the game was on the line. Arsenal won, but they did so in a manner that contravened the notion of sportsmanship. At the end of the game the Arsenal manager Arsene Wenger apologized and offered Sheffield United a replay, which they accepted. An even more remarkable event occurred a few months later in a game involving West Ham: while the opposition keeper was badly injured, a West Ham player crossed the ball to Paolo di Canio who, instead of heading it into the unguarded net, caught the ball and pointed to the injured player. In both cases obvious self-interest was rejected in favour of a set of residual principles, clustered around the notion of sportsmanship and fair play.

Footballers acquired, as part of their habitus, a deep-seated attachment to the principle of sporting behaviour. In other words, a 'true sportsperson' will adhere, in words, thoughts, beliefs and actions, to the kinds of values demonstrated by Arsene Wenger (in agreeing to a replay) and Paolo di Canio (in refusing to take advantage of an injured opponent). Now the values exhibited by these two were virtually extinct: the fact that they elicited such widespread comment and praise demonstrates this. Managers, players, agents, spectators and journalists typically operate, on a practical level, without regard to a sporting ethos, while maintaining a discursive commitment to it; we could say that it is like a Gricean cooperative principle, a set of ideals against which the field and its activities can be measured, judged and critiqued. As Bourdieu explains, while the Gricean principle 'is constantly flouted' it functions as 'a kind of implicit presupposition of all conversation . . . which, though it is constantly transgressed, can be evoked at any time, as a reminder of the tacitly accepted rule or an implicit reference to what a conversation has to be in order to be a real dialogue' (2000: 122). The sporting ethos survives precisely because the field is unthinkable without it, and concomitantly because it is the foundation of sport-as-commodity for media and business interests.

The inflection, and eventual transformation, of the field of sport by the discourses and imperatives of media and business has been a gradual process, although it clearly accelerated during the second half of the twentieth century. In the mid-nineteenth century sport was located, in Bourdieu's (1993) terms, at the autonomous pole of the field of cultural production. Bourdieu writes that:

> The field of cultural production . . . owes its . . . structure to the opposition between the field of restricted production as a system of producing cultural goods . . . for a public of producers of cultural goods, and the field of large-scale cultural production, specifically organized with a view to the production of cultural goods destined for non-producers . . . 'the public at large'. In contrast to the field of large-scale cultural production, which submits to the laws of competition for the conquest of the largest possible market, the field of restricted production tends to develop its own criteria for the evaluation of its products, thus achieving the truly cultural recognition accorded by the peer group whose members are both privileged clients and competitors. (115)

Bourdieu is writing about the literary field in France during the first half of the nineteenth century, but the observations and principles are equally applicable to the incipient field of sport. That field was set up by, and oriented towards, an exclusive group that produced the discourses, institutions, competitions, rules, techniques, forms of knowledge and bodily practices that were exchanged among, and formed the basis of ongoing competition between, members. The field of restricted production is predicated on separation from the influence or interference of other fields (and their discourses and imperatives), and from the wider socio-cultural field, what Bourdieu refers to as the 'public at large' (115). It is relatively autonomous, in that it has the power:

> to define its own criteria for the production and evaluation of its products. This implies translation of all external determinations in conformity with its own principles of functioning. Thus, the more cultural producers form a closed field of competition for cultural legitimacy, the more the internal demarcations appear irreducible to any external factors of economic, political or social differentiation. (115)

Moreover, whereas many sectors of the field of restricted production owe their autonomy to their lack of commercial value, or their irrelevance to other powerful fields, from the beginning sport was derived from, aligned with, and served the ends of, the field of power. Sport as a field was constituted out of a strong class-based disavowal of, and disengagement from, both commercial imperatives and the needs and interests of the dominated classes; and one of its primary functions was to manifest this separation as a marker of what Bourdieu (1989) calls cultural 'distinction'.

Conclusion

Discursive disjunctions and contradictions characterized the incipient field of sport. It started out, in its earliest folk incarnations, as a form of play; in the eighteenth and early nineteenth century it was institutionalized and popularized, and embraced professionalism and commercialism; in the mid-nineteenth century it had become closely aligned and associated with the discourses and values of public school athletics and Victorian notions of fair play. In the following chapter we will give an account of how the founding discourses of sport transformed a quite diverse set of folk games and forms of play into a 'a major cultural achievement of the Victorian era' (Hargreaves 1987: 45), and eventually into a global cultural form; and how they took on a significant socio-cultural status and work, most particularly with regard to the production of normative gender performances and templates.

CHAPTER TWO

Play and sport

Introduction

During the 1980s and 1990s Nike produced a series of television advertisements, now widely posted and available on You Tube, that attempted to take advantage of their commercial relationship with the Brazilian national football team. As with most forms and genres of contemporary audio-visual advertising, there were two main imperatives at work here: the first was to gain and maintain the audience's attention; and the second was to produce an association, in the mind of the audience, between Nike the sporting goods company and a particular form of cultural value, in this case a style of football – the Brazilian way of playing. The Nike advertisements that feature Brazil tend to emphasize that team's tradition of valuing what we might call skilful, non-ends-directed football, in contrast to national teams such as Germany, England and even Italy and Argentina, which have usually adopted a more instrumental approach to the game. Until repeated failures at the World Cup in the 1970s and 1980s caused something of a change of heart and tactics. It was said of Brazil that that they would rather 'play beautifully and lose' than resort to 'ugly' football (playing defensively, systematic fouling).

One of those advertisements is set in an anonymous airport lounge, with the players (Ronaldino, Romario, Denilson and other lesser names and faces) in transit, travelling from or to an international game. They are trying, rather unsuccessfully, to kill time: they make phone calls, attempt to get some sleep, read distractedly or just lounge about looking bored. Then Ronaldino opens his kit bag, produces a football and starts to play – kicking, dribbling, heading and balancing the ball. The others quickly and enthusiastically join in, and a game develops. It is not a serious game, or a game played by football rules: it is a Brazilian game-as-play, based on conjuring something out of nothing, with the intentions being both to amuse and indulge oneself – while also entertaining, showing off for and outperform the others in terms of skill, tricks, touch and creativity.

Football as play breaks out within the space of the airport lounge, which serves as a kind of metaphor for the routine emptiness and nothingness of everyday life, but perhaps also for the contemporary state of football understood as a businesslike, bureaucratic and joyless job. As soon as the football starts bouncing about, the players become animated: their bodies 'wake up', their faces smile, they are energized. Bureaucratic officialdom, in the shape of an airport security officer, tries to bring a halt to proceedings by grabbing the ball – the golden rule of airports being 'thou shalt not play here'. However, the players kick the ball from out of his hands, and continue. To the tune of a samba, the play moves in and out of passengers, technology and more airport 'referees', until Ronaldino remembers that football is also about scoring goals. He balances, steadies, shoots – and hits a metal queuing post standing in as one of the goalposts.

Sporting advertisements usually condense the field – its stars, stories, drama, crowd excitement and skills – into a few visuals. A football commercial involving a star such as Ronaldino would normally show him avoiding tackles and displaying his skills, and then scoring the winning goal; it would also probably show the celebrations of the players, and the fans shouting and screaming with joy. In this way the name of the sponsor would be associated with the action, the players and the gear, but also with the passion, excitement and beauty of football. This advertisement is different and, in a quite interesting way, it doesn't emphasize the game, but what is behind the game, its irreducible core of play. Here football isn't just the institutionally authorized practices associated with and organized by the field of sport. The implicit message is that the strong influence that media and corporate values, logics and interests (including, of course, Nike's) exert over football is disposed to kill off the magic, the spontaneity, the sheer exuberance, invention, individuality and fun associated with playing. However, the advertisement is saying that no matter how much commercial and bureaucratic discourses and logics attempt to banish play, it always returns when you least expect it: football is alive and well, spontaneous and fun, because the disposition to play never leaves it. The commercially and bureaucratically inflected field of sport attempts to curb or limit the wastefulness and transgression of play (represented by the airport security people trying to steal the ball away), but play continues to break out because it offers a form of escape and joy that continues to work on and through players and spectators.

There are no definitive theoretical accounts or explanations of play; however, there are bodies of work which are useful in helping us make sense of play, as both a concept and a discourse. In this chapter, we'll provide an account of the theories and explanations of play put forward by George Bataille, Johan Huizinga and Roger Caillois, and consider how and why the discourse of play continues to exert a strong influence over the field of sport.

Play and general economy

A footballer who juggles the ball in the middle of a game for no apparent reason or benefit, a cricketer who suddenly starts parodying the bowling action of other players, a ice hockey fan selecting and trading players in a fantasy league: all these activities can be understood in terms of what George Bataille refers to as a 'general economy', defined as 'a play of energy which no end limits' (1991: 23). Bataille differentiates general economy from what he calls 'specific economic systems', which are 'particular operations with limited ends' (22). The set of activities referred to above come under the category of a general economy because the energy expended appears to have no systematic or rational utility; in other words any potential gains associated with them (juggling the ball might enhance the player's football skills, winning the fantasy league could constitute a form of cultural capital) are inadequate or incommensurate with regard to conventional economic logics. The necessary articulation that is presumed, within a closed economy, between expenditure and growth is not really applicable in those activities. General economy, on the other hand, offers an entirely different explanation with regard to the question of expenditure, one that is predicated not on gain but on loss:

> As soon as we act reasonably we want to consider the utility of our actions; utility implies . . . a maintenance of growth. Now if it is necessary to respond to exuberance, it is no doubt possible to use it for growth. But . . . supposing there is no longer any growth possible, what is to be done with the seething energy that remains? To waste it is obviously not to use it. And yet, what we have is a draining-away, a pure and simple loss, which occurs in any case: from the first, the excess energy, if it cannot be used for growth, is lost. (30–1)

In some ways general economy is similar to the notion of power, in that they are abstractions which manifest themselves as traces and effects, and are best apprehended in terms of the work they perform. This notion of a necessary and wasted expenditure of energy fits in neatly with, and offers a convenient point of origin for considering, the disposition to play. Bataille's contention that 'life starts only with the deficit of . . . systems . . . order and reserve has meaning only from the moment the ordered and reserved forces liberate and lose themselves for ends that cannot be subordinated to anything one can account for' (1989: 128) is commensurate with the notion of play as pleasure-in-escape from the everyday, from boredom, and from social restrictions and routines. One aspect of general economy that is particularly relevant to our understanding of the disposition to play is the phenomenon of potlatch. Bataille's reading of potlatch (best characterized as a systematic and apparently pointless destroying or gifting of wealth) is that it is a loss (something is wasted) that appears to be a disguised utility (it is not done in isolation, but in front of others, which means that the one suffering the loss acquires capital) that is in fact a disguised loss (nothing is really produced and energy is wasted, but the imperatives of the closed economy appear to be adhered to). The value of potlatch, for Bataille and theorists of play such as Huizinga and Caillois, is that it is an obvious example of the community being played, rather than the other way round; in other words, although the community may produce all kinds of explanations, rationales and narratives about potlatch that insist upon and explain its utility, these are merely discursive performatives that satisfy the imperatives associated with closed economies.

Play, from this perspective, is a disposition that inhabits or passes through sites, in different forms and intensities and at different times, but which is often discursively produced as, and recuperated in terms of, narratives of individual or communal agency and utility. This is important because theorists of play such as Huizinga and Caillois specifically and resolutely define it as a non-productive activity, even while allowing that the question of what constitutes utility is highly problematical. So if we return to the Nike commercial we can say that Ronaldo, Roberto Carlos and the others indulge themselves in footballing tricks, acts of display and an expenditure of energy that clearly stand outside the order of a closed economy (they will soon have to play important, competitive game of football with national and individual prestige at stake, not to mention the financial rewards that go to the winner). However, the concepts of agency and utility cannot account for the moments of madness when professional footballers turn into children.

Homo Ludens

The notion that play inhabits and animates cultural practices, and constitutes a strong presence even in its apparent absence, is central to the thesis of Huizinga's *Homo Ludens* (1966). Huizinga characterizes play as both a universal abstraction (he posits that it is not only prior to culture – it effectively animates it) and a historically situated disposition-as-practice that is:

> older than culture (and) . . . more than a mere physiological phenomenon or a psychological reflex . . . It is a significant function . . . that is to say, there is some sense to it. In play there is something 'at play' which transcends the immediate needs of life and imparts meaning to the action. All play means something. If we call the active principle that makes up the essence of play 'instinct', we explain nothing. (1)

This quote identifies two fundamental characteristics of play. First, it 'is a thing of its own' (3): it has no biological purpose, does not 'serve something which is not play' (2) and is possessed of its own generic qualities. It gives rise to an infinite number of socio-cultural manifestations and transformations, but always within a strictly limited regime of characteristics, imperatives and qualities. Second, although play has no moral or ethical function, it is both a catalyst for imaginative activity and stands in opposition to a mood or culture of seriousness. That play is opposed to seriousness does not mean, however, that it cannot be an intense activity: the disposition to play has the capacity to possess people and move them out of or away from their everyday duties and responsibilities. As well as being self-serving and opposed to seriousness, play has, for Huizinga, six other generic aspects: it is voluntary or freely adopted; disinterested and irreducible to any utility; distinct or sequestered from ordinary life; creates and demands adherence to order (through the adoption of rules or patterns of behaviour); operates under temporal and spatial limits; and is either representational or competitive in some respect. Huizinga provides elaborate descriptions, definitions and examples of what he means by these terms, but the key to reading, explicating and grounding play-as-practice is his argument that, from the nineteenth century on, play atrophies (198).

It is easier to recognize more precisely what Huizinga means by play, and to reconcile the apparent contradictions in his accounts of it, once we know what kinds of socio-historical forces, tendencies and cultural forms 'send it away'. One of the most significant of these cultural forms is modern sport:

> Now, with the increasing systematisation and regimentation of sport, something of the pure play-quality is inevitably lost . . . In modern social life sport occupies a place alongside and apart from the cultural process . . . The ability of modern social techniques to stage mass demonstrations with the maximum of outward show in the field of athletics does not alter the fact that neither the Olympiads nor the organized sports of American Universities nor the loudly trumpeted international contests have, in the smallest degree, raised sport to the level of a culture-creating activity. However important it may be for players or spectators, it remains sterile. The old play-factor has undergone almost complete atrophy. (197–8)

There are three factors in Huizinga's account of modern sport that differentiate it from play, and the first and by far the most important of these is that it is derived from a world-view that is essentially utilitarian and rationalist. In Huizinga's account of play and its generic characteristics, play is of-and-for-itself, rather than a means to an end. However, while play may take itself seriously, it does not extend that privilege – a rejection that is reciprocated by a utilitarian mindset. Everything follows from this, and clears a path between play and sport. The ambiguities found in Huizinga's use of terms such as 'competition', 'free and voluntary', and 'temporal and spatial limitations' become clearer once we contextualize them within one order of discourse or another. Football players may take the field voluntarily, but if the dominant motivation behind their play is financial gain or to improve their fitness, then they are not playing. Similarly, although there are spatial and temporal limitations to a kick-about among players in a park (they may tacitly agree to take turns in kicking, one may act as goalkeeper while the others take shots, shots at goal should be from about the edge of the penalty area), that is a very different situation from the necessary adherence, on the part of professional footballers, to the exact iterations and regularities articulated in a FIFA rulebook.

For Huizinga, two main factors – capitalism and political instrumentalism – contribute to this differentiation of play from sport; however, although both are clearly derived from a utilitarian/rationalist world-view, they take different socio-cultural forms. The economies of time and effort that go into the creation and maintenance of the play–civilization nexus are theoretically untenable within a capitalist order: if time is money, there is no place for the unproductive use of time. With political instrumentalism we are dealing with different dispositions, logics and imperatives. When Huizinga writes about 'the ability of modern social techniques to stage mass demonstrations with the maximum of outward show in the field of athletics' (1966: 198), he is clearly referring to political spectacles such as the 1936 Berlin Olympics: here the investment of time and effort in rituals is paramount, but the point or ends of such an investment is the accumulation of prestige, the maintenance of power, and the training and disciplining of bodies and minds.

The account of play that Huizinga produces in *Homo Ludens* is both socio-historical and mythical: play has an ahistorical golden age, which is undone by the forces of capitalism, government and modernity. The problem with this account, in which play more or less succumbs to, and is atrophied by, historical forces and developments, is that it contradicts Huizinga's own contention that 'civilisation is . . . played . . . it arises in and as play, and never leaves it' (1966: 173). What is implied here is that play is a disposition that inhabits not just people and places but, as Huizinga admits, world-views and institutions that are entirely antithetical to it. He devotes a small section of *Homo Ludens* to a discussion of business as play, but never seriously pursues the line of enquiry that capitalism might be characterized by or associated with a sense of play.

Play and games

This contradiction in Huizinga's account of play is picked up and addressed by Roger Caillois in *Men, Play and Games* (2001). Caillois provides a systematic categorization of play-as-genre, divided into different forms (*agon*, *alea*, *ilinx*, mimicry, which correspond roughly to the institutions of sport, gambling, festivals/carnival and shows) and poles (at one extreme we have *ludus*, where rules and conventions dominate, and at the other *paidea*, which is improvised and even anarchic). He extends Huizinga's work by demonstrating how play, which he defines as being in opposition to and of a different order from institutionalized socio-cultural activities, comes to be 'two things at once': it is simultaneously that which is official and serious, and an antithetical disposition which cannot be reinscribed or reincorporated within a discursive regime of utility. Caillois insists that play is 'an occasion of pure waste' (2001: 5), even as it operates within a wider setting or context where financial and other forms of capital can be exchanged:

> Play . . . creates no wealth or goods, thus differing from work or art . . . play is an occasion of pure waste: waste of time, energy, ingenuity, skill, and often of money . . . Play must be defined as a free and voluntary activity, a source of joy and amusement. A game which one would be forced to play . . . would become constraint . . . from which one would strive to be free. As an obligation or simply an order, it would lose one of its basic characteristics: the fact that the player devotes himself spontaneously to the game, of his free will and for his own pleasure, each time completely free to choose retreat, silence, meditation, idle solitude, or creative activity . . . (play occurs) only when the players have a desire to play . . . in order to find diversion, escape from responsibility and routine . . . In effect play is essentially a separate occupation, carefully isolated from the rest of life. (5–6)

For Caillois authentic play is separated off from most areas of ordinary life for two reasons. First, it is non-productive: art does not count as play because it produces material goods, which can also function as commodities or as inalienable cultural forms. Second, it is volitional: professional sportspersons are working, not playing. However, he recognizes that those material and historical contexts of ordinary life (the workplace, post-industrial society) are not only both what is being escaped from, but also potentially the sites of escape. So while the casino or race track are part of the wider field of capitalism, not all the activities that take place there, nor the motivations of the players, are explicable in terms of a capitalist regime or logic. Gambling, for instance:

> remains completely unproductive. The sum of the winnings at best would only equal the losses of other players. Nearly always the winnings are less, because of large overheads, taxes, and other profits of the entrepreneur. He alone does not play, or if he plays he is protected against loss by the law of averages. In effect, he is the only one who cannot take pleasure in gambling. (5)

We find much the same situation when we consider the Nike commercial and the situation it represents. We noted that the narrative seems to be suggesting that although play and sport are related, they are not exactly synonymous: the chaotic activity that erupts in the airport lounge is quintessential play (it is volitional, wasteful, separated from ordinary life, creative and clearly escapist), but when Brazil has to play a competitive match the demands of the real, institutionalized game clearly belongs in the category of work. However, even this apparently neat differentiation needs to be qualified. There is a great deal of financial, social and bureaucratic pressure that militates against the same players reverting to playful (and wasteful) behaviour once they are on the field; in other words, play normally cannot break out when and where the players are subject to surveillance, since it requires some level of physical or temporal separation from institutional scrutiny. If players started performing, repeatedly and openly, in a non-utilitarian and wasteful manner, they would probably be substituted, ridiculed by the media and fans, and perhaps even find themselves subject to legal action (they could be accused of throwing the game). The field and its institutions would ensure that what was perceived as consistently wasteful and self-indulgent play would have serious consequences.

However, there are a number of examples of the phenomenon of wasteful play inhabiting professional English and world football: Rodney Marsh of Queens Park Rangers and Matt Le Tissier of Southampton were favourites with the fans, although often berated by managers and sports analysts, because of their penchant for 'playing' to a different logic than that of the team. Both were highly skilful – but idiosyncratic – players who found it difficult to fit into game plans and rarely did the workmanlike tasks their managers expected of them (tackling back or helping out the defence when the team was under pressure, not taking risks in tight situations). They could score spectacular goals, and were capable, on their day, of winning a game on their own; but they are often remembered for their non-utilitarian contributions (juggling the ball in the middle of an intensely competitive game; making an opponent look stupid by beating him more than once). International football examples include the Columbian goalkeeper Rene Higueta, who once let a shot sail over his head so he could mule-kick it from behind his back, and the Bulgarian international Dimitar Yakimov who, in the middle of a 1966 World Cup game against Brazil, went off on a mazy dribble that took him past player after player (sometimes twice) to absolutely no effect, save for the obvious pleasure of doing it.

If we follow this line of thinking a little further we can find numerous other examples of the field of professional sport and its spaces, ostensibly defined, delineated and ruled by the logic of commoditization or consumption, being used for the purposes of play – and not just by the players. There is the relatively recent phenomenon of fans dressing up in extravagant, eccentric or colourful costumes and so adding to the spectacle of the occasion; the Wellington Sevens rugby competition is better known for its crowd performances than it is for its sport. These activities are commensurate with and are driven by the logic of sport-as-capitalism; following a team or wanting to be part of a sporting spectacle requires people to become consumers both in direct (buying tickets to the game, hiring costumes) and tangential (transport costs, meals and drinks) ways. However, just as professional footballers are not always necessarily workers, so spectators are not simply consumers: they usually go to games of their own volition, gain no advantage, are separated off and escape from the ordinary world, and engage intensely and creatively with the material at hand (players, officials, other members of the crowd).

Play as cultural practice

Caillois' work is valuable in the way it explores and addresses the relationship between the disposition to play and the socio-cultural fields, sites and spaces in which this disposition is both clearly manifested and to some extent discursively authorized. That is one of the more significant issues raised by the Nike advertisement: there is a reconciliation and articulation between wasteful play and the utilitarian duties, responsibilities and habitus of the professional sportsperson because play has an abiding, inalienable and even foundational value within the field; to deny play would be to deny the discursive base of the field of sport. There is also the question of the extent to which play can still inhabit those authorized sites and places within sport (the football field, the crowd) which are ruled by, and seemingly only explicable within, the imperatives and logics of a specific economy. Michel de Certeau addresses this issue, in a general way, in *The Practice of Everyday Life* (1988): he posits a series of binaries, such as place/space and strategies/tactics, as a means of characterizing the relationship between valorized and authoritative institutions and their agents, and those who are, precisely because of power differentials, obliged to perform compliance with regard to those official regimes. So a factory, bureaucracy, church or a professional sports team are all simultaneously places (maintained and guaranteed by networks of power and capital, and able to dictate or negotiate the rules of practice to those who deal with and inhabit them) and spaces (which is what a place becomes when it is put to unofficial uses, such as an employee making trades within a fantasy sport league on a computer during work time). Places make use of strategies, what Certeau describes as 'the calculus of force-relationship', which becomes possible when an institution attains relative autonomy within and 'can be isolated from an environment' (1988: xix). Spaces, on the other hand, are inhabited by tactics or calculations 'which cannot count on a spatial or institutional location' (xix). The disposition to play manifests itself across all cultural fields, most of which are disinclined to accept or tolerate it on its own terms.

There are some places (the family, childcare centres) where play of-and-for-itself is not only allowed but even encouraged, but these fields and contexts are mainly associated with groups who are largely exempt from incorporation into the logic of a closed economy. There are times and places that are set aside for play across the wider socio-cultural field (weekends and holidays; sports fields and resorts), but this regimentation of the times and sites of play is antithetical to the notion of play as spontaneous and volitional. Cultural fields and institutions that are characterized by a discursive commitment to or identification with play (such as sport) host play on their own terms, both explicitly (there are strict rules and regulations regarding the movements and activities of spectators), and implicitly (the orchestration of 'spontaneous' behaviour on the part of crowds). In this regulated environment, play is very much like Certeau's tactic that 'insinuates itself into the other's place, fragmentarily, without taking it over in its entirety, without being able to keep it at a distance' (xix). If play is forced to operate in another place, that is to say within fields and sites that endeavour to colonize it, then two things become apparent. First, play necessarily takes on forms that would seem, from the perspectives offered by Huizinga and Caillois, to constitute its antithesis (work, capitalism, bureaucratic regimentation). Second and concomitantly, the places supposedly operating within the logic of a closed economy are not what they seem – they are sites and spaces of waste and dissipation. Allen Guttmann points out that:

> Moments of play appear unpredictably in the most unlikely places, even upon the gallows . . . In the film *Cool Hand Luke*, a group of convicts bewilders the guards by increasing the tempo of their road-work, by running back and forth in eager performance of their imposed tasks, by laughing, by turning punishment into play . . . Had the convicts begun the game purely for their own amusement . . . the activity would have been . . . indistinguishable from the utilitarian work that was done. (1978: 13–14)

This imbrication of play with sites of utility leads to the question of whether it is possible to distinguish play at all. Some forms of play remove themselves, materially, temporally and psychologically, from contexts that intrude upon play's volitional nature, which is the point of the Nike advertisement: there may be minor negative consequences for playing in the bureaucratic spaces of the airport (a fine, a ticking off), but they are considerably less severe than if the disposition to play (wastefully) was to break out in the middle of a World Cup game between Brazil and Argentina. But rather than distinguish between the generic features of play and certain contexts (work, professionalism, institutionalism), it is more useful to analyse the relationship between play as a disposition and genre, and the different socio-cultural uses to which it is continually being put.

Arjun Appadurai makes the point that it is impossible to state that things and practices definitively 'belong to' the category of gift or commodity, precisely because they continue to circulate, and are appropriated and reinterpreted, within different socio-cultural contexts. Commodities, for instance, have no definitive status, but can be understood as:

> things in a certain situation, a situation that can characterise many different kinds of thing, at different points in their social lives. This means looking at the commodity potential of all things rather than searching fruitlessly for the magic distinction between commodities and other sorts of things . . . But how are we to define the commodity situation? I propose that the commodity situation in the social life of any 'thing' be defined as the situation in which its exchangeability (past, present, or future) for some other thing is its socially relevant feature. (Appadurai 1988: 13)

We can do much the same with play, and suggest that something is in a play situation or phase when its socially relevant features are commensurate with the imperatives and generic characteristics outlined by Huizinga and Caillois, rather than with those of antithetical regimes (such as capitalism, in which case exchangeability would be its socially relevant feature). But while play has its own generic features, this is not the same as saying that it has (had) a stable meaning: if the manifestations of and the disposition to play move in and out of the commodity situation, for instance, then one person's escape will become another person's profit, and vice versa. Moreover, in a cultural field such as sport where play has a significant discursive status (e.g. play is clearly central to sport's foundation narrative) but is at odds with dominant forms of capital (those of the media or business), its meanings and functions are likely to be relatively contingent and the subject of (non-playful) competition, and even symbolic violence. So rather than understanding sport as having been animated, at some historical point, by a now atrophied ludic disposition, we can think of it as a set of sites which, despite the influence exerted upon it by governments, media and capitalism, continues (necessarily) to value, provoke and provide occasions for the disposition to play.

The discursive legacy of play

The field of sport has always emphasized and benefited from the discursive legacy of play; but it is also a discursive presence as something that is superseded but remains within the fabric of the new form:

> [S]ports to one or other degree embody an irreducible element of play. Play is a type of activity having no intrinsic purpose or end, and as such it is a form of activity which enjoys a universal appeal. Sports

> play is not always unalloyed by other motives or considerations .
> . . and in specific instances (politicized and professional sport, for
> example) play may be by no means the most important element. But
> the ludic impulse is, nevertheless, always present to some degree
> at least, existing in tension with disciplined, organized aspects of
> sporting activity . . . sports play tends to be highly formalized . . .
> Rule-structured play, like play in general, 'suspends reality', but in
> this case through the acceptance of formal codes ordering the use of
> space, time and general behaviour . . . both participants and onlookers
> are indulging in a form of 'play-acting', and in this respect the activity
> can be said to be 'unserious' or set aside from normal life. (Holt 1989:
> 10–11)

Sport has tended to represent itself as sequestered and utopian: both a world
within itself and a kind of exemplar of what the wider world should be
like; hence those Olympic posters that promote the games as a vehicle for
global harmony, tolerance and understanding. However, it also occupies
a special place in the wider social field, largely because it is associated
with and animated by the disposition to play. So the contemporary field of
sport is predicated both upon an ethos (concerning disinterestedness, fair
play, participation, self-overcoming) and an anti-utilitarian escapism (play
as the pleasure of wasting time). In its current manifestation, however,
it is dominated (both at discursive and practical levels) by the media-as-
business, and concomitantly subject and given over to commercial logics
and imperatives.

How do performances within the field of sport, and the sporting habitus
that inflects them, reflect and embody this disjunction? The strong influence
the media-as-business exerts over sport should effectively foreclose the
notion that sport is either an ethos or value, or a form of play. At the same
time, play remains part of the habitus of the field, and it can never entirely
or successfully be made to disappear; as one of the foundational discourses
of the field of sport, it is associated with, and can always be turned into,
cultural capital. The Rumanian tennis player Ilie Nastase drew crowds
partly because he has a great player, but also because he usually 'put on
a performance'. Nastase's theatrics (hiding on the court to avoid an angry
opponent or official censure, and like a character in a pantomime, urging
the crowd to misdirect his pursuers) had nothing to do with results; rather
they expressed a desire to escape from the tedium of sporting activity
understood as a job, another 'day at the office'. It is paradox that sport
has taken on such a significant socio-cultural status and popularity only
because it was originally, and remains to some extent, a form of play. The
space and time of play is seductive, in that it appears to be about nothing at
all, and constitutes an active avoidance of the world and all its seriousness,
regimentation and order.

There have been a number of videos posted on You Tube, including one produced by the Italian Football Federation that emphasis the ludic, non-serious and sporting character of football. The video ('Football Is Fair Play') starts with scenes of player violence (fouls, head butts, elbows, pushing and shoving) and fan disruptions (riots, missiles being thrown, flares on the field) against a background of threatening and discordant noise. This gives way to an upbeat, samba-inflected hip-hop song, and the scenes of the crowd at play and enjoying itself: dancing, singing, wearing colourful costumes and playing musical instruments. The next scene is of professional footballers walking out with children, which functions as a discursive reminder of the origins of competitive football – the child at play. Although the rest of the video is more concerned with the ethics of fair play (showing players adhering to the spirit of the game), it also implicitly reaffirms the relation between play and the ethos of the game: when players refuse to take advantage of a bad call that has gone their way, they are effectively performing a commitment to something both different from and more than the bureaucratic apparatus (the rules) of professional football.

Conclusion

The disposition to play served as a catalyst for British folk games, and those chaotic and local activities in turn served as the templates of and departure points for the creation of the formalized, standardized and bureaucratized games that constituted the field of sport. In the mid-nineteenth-century British public schools recognized that play could be used to help facilitate work, specifically in replicating the conditions and sites of what Foucault refers to as discipline. The formal disinterestedness of public school athletics was both commensurate with and fed off the form and sensibility of play. The performance of non-seriousness was not antithetical, for instance, to the notion of competition; what was important in public school sport was to throw yourself into the fight, while at the same time remaining sufficiently detached so as not to be seen to be trying too hard. The thing itself (winning, the prize of victory) was subordinate, and could never be allowed, to become an end in itself.

The continuity and parallel between play and sport as spaces where reality is suspended carried two further benefits. First, it allowed sport, which was from its beginning heavily informed by and committed to socio-political work (the maintenance and normalization of various forms of symbolic violence carried out at the levels of class, race, gender, sexual preference), to carry out this work in a covert, and therefore much more effective, manner, because sport necessarily articulated itself as 'without regard to' any form of political, social or cultural preference or bias. Second, it's attraction as a place where the world could be escaped from, and the body liberated from surveillance and constraints, made it an ideal place to inculcate, normalize, train, teach and discipline:

> It is because sport is so 'obviously' physical . . . concerned with the body, governed by natural laws, which function irrespective of what the observer thinks or feels about them, that it can be claimed to have nothing to do with politics or society . . . Yet sport is no more or less 'natural' than any other activity in which we indulge collectively. (Hargreaves 1987: 142)

A corollary to this is that the lure of sport as escape, as an idealized place that surpasses and takes us away from the boredom, drudgery and institutionalized unfairness and inequality of everyday life, made it highly attractive not just to the schoolboys of public schools, but to the widest possible demographic. We will address this issue in more detail later in the next chapter.

CHAPTER THREE

Public school athletics

Introduction

Where and when does the field of sport, and the ideas and discourses that animated it, begin? Consider the following passage from Richard Holt's *Sport and the British* (1989), which refers to the attitudes and practices that characterized late Victorian public schools:

> Whereas boys who loved sports might have been pronounced 'idle' by earlier generations, Victorian schoolmasters were inclined to reserve that word for those who did not care for games. 'Any lower boy in this house who does not play football once a day and twice on half holiday will be fined half a crown and kicked', read a notice at Eton, whose headmaster from 1884 until 1905 was Edmond Warre, a former Fellow of All Souls whose enthusiasm for the classics was only surpassed by his dedication to the Eight. (76)

Like many other traditions that were introduced in the Victorian period, the status of sport and games as being integral to English national character and culture was a fiction that traced its origins back to conveniently idealized times and places; in this case Thomas Arnold's Rugby School, and before that the agonistic festivals of classical Greece, which partly explains why so many classical scholars were also sports enthusiasts. In fact as many sports' scholars are at pains to point out (Hargreaves 1987; Holt 1989; Mangan 1981), Thomas Arnold had no interest in games, being completely 'insensitive to the possibilities of an athletic ethos with team games as the instrument of moral conditioning' (Mangan 1981: 16); and up until the middle of the century there seems to have been at least as much antipathy towards games as there was support, both at public schools and within the universities (Holt 1989). This changed radically after 1850: the 'increased number of boarding-schools helped the development of games', and the 'acceptance of organised sport as an important part of school life was now shared by headmasters of old and new establishments alike' (Money 1997: 66).

What were the circumstances that contributed to this transformation? The period from the 1820s to the 1840s saw numbers drop dramatically in most public schools because of their 'obvious defects – the barbaric living conditions, the narrow syllabus, the neglect of religion, and the gross indiscipline' (Money 1997: 64). However, the rise of a new, wealthy middle class had 'created a widening demand for education, especially boarding education' (Mangan 1981: 15). Arnold was the first to take advantage of this situation, restoring the 'soiled and tattered reputation of the public schools' and reassuring the 'new middle-class clientele that their sons would be safe in his bosom' (15). So at one level Arnold and the system that followed him took on the task of educating the rising middle class and integrating them into the (previously aristocratic) dominant social fabric. Allied to this was a second, and equally important, contemporary class-based context and utility, predicated on the social unrest manifested in the Charterist movement and the wider 'socialistic claims of the oppressed' (Hargreaves 1987: 39). In these circumstances Britain needed leadership from 'Christian gentlemen, men who were disciplined, socially responsible and self-reliant enough, not only to govern themselves but the lower orders as well' (39).

The civilizing process

These changes within public schools, and by extension the development of sport, were part of what Norbert Elias (2000) refers to as a wider 'civilizing process' that characterized and influenced English society, history and politics in the eighteenth and nineteenth centuries. He argues that it was a factor in the outlawing, controlling or modifying of blood sports in the eighteenth century, through direct means such as legislation, and indirect ones such as the codification and ritualization of fox-hunting. Elias and Dunning write that with regard to hunting, its earlier forms:

> imposed on their followers few restraints. People enjoyed the pleasure of hunting and killing animals in whatever way they could . . . Sometimes masses of animals were driven near the hunters so they could enjoy the pleasures of killing without too much exertion. For the higher ranking social cadres, the excitement of hunting and killing animals had always been to some extent the peacetime equivalent of the excitement connected with killing humans in times of war. (1993: 161)

The influence of the civilizing process transformed the way hunting was understood and played out, a change manifested in both the elaborate ritualizing of fox-hunting and the forms of pleasure it gave rise to:

> A glance back at the earlier forms of hunting shows the peculiarities of English fox-hunting in better perspective. It was a form of hunting in which the hunters imposed on themselves and their hounds a number of highly specific restraints. The whole organization of fox-hunting, the behaviour of the participants, the training of the hounds, was governed by an extremely elaborate code . . . Fox-hunting gentlemen killed, as it were, by proxy – by delegating the task of killing to the hounds . . . (and) part of the enjoyment of hunting become a visual enjoyment; the pleasure derived from doing it had been transformed into the pleasure of seeing it done. (161–2)

As Elias and Dunning suggest, one of the 'crucial problems confronting society in the course of the civilizing process' was that of finding a 'new balance between pleasure and restraint', which led to the 'progressive tightening of regulating controls over people's behaviour and the corresponding conscience-formation', particularly with regard to the 'internalisation of rules that regulate more elaborately all spheres of life' (165). This process had both a moral and an economic dimension. It was moral in the sense that is was predicated on the belief that the subordination of life to the principles of rationality and reason was progressive, and could bring about the improvement of human society and nature. It was economic in the sense that the application of rationality to human behaviour was considered to be essentially beneficial and productive, that it helped eliminate wasteful expenditure of the mind, body, resources, energy and time.

From play to rationality

The differences between a rationalist and a non-rationalist discursive form is particularly demonstrable if we can consider how the relation between play, time and space underwent a dramatic transformation in the move from folk games to public school and Victorian sport. Folk sport was part of the process whereby the relation between people and world was ritualized. However, as Bakhtin has demonstrated, those activities belonged to carnival, which while it occupied religious time and space, was:

> shaped according to a certain pattern of play . . . Carnival is not a spectacle seen by the people; they live it, and everyone participates because its very idea embraces all the people. While carnival lasts, there is no other life outside it. During carnival time life is subject only to its laws . . . the laws of its freedom. (1984: 70)

In folk football the disposition to play manifested itself as waste, transgression, and an opposition to dominant and conventional regimes of power:

> At harvest festival in the Upper Wye valley, Francis Kilvert observed what sounds like traditional football in 1871: 'After dinner all the men played or rather kicked football at each other and then it grew dark, when the game ended in a general royal scuffle or scrummage.' Interrogating an old resident of Langley Burrell in Wiltshire, Kilvert discovered football had survived the sabbatarian efforts of the Revd. Samuel Ashe . . . who 'used to come round quietly under the trees and bide his time till the football came near him when he would catch up the ball and pierce the bladder with a pin. But some of the young fellows would be even with the parson for they would bring a spare bladder, blow it, and soon have the football flying again. (Holt 1989: 39)

The public schools brought a different concept of, and relation to, the time of play. Folk football was closely tied to the religious calendar:

> For most of their history, the Christmas and Easter holidays, like most other festivals, had their own distinctive sporting characters . . . the main competitive sport was football, in one or other of its forms. Communal contests, like that at Kirkham in Lancashire, often took place on Christmas day itself. Christmas day football was played over the whole of the British Isles. In Scotland, at Scone, the married men strove against the bachelors, while at Inveresk the wives tackled the spinsters. Hardy Scots fishwives took to golf on any holiday . . . Easter sport usually had both more variety and greater sobriety. It could embrace virtually any competitive activity . . . from quoits, bowls, bell-ringing, and cock-fighting. (Brailsford 1991: 3)

Public school sport, games and activities, on the other hand, were secular, bureaucratized, institutionalized, and rather than serving as an alternative 'out of time' and form of escape from everyday time, they became the everyday. The freedom and spontaneity of carnival time was replaced by mechanized, standardized and organized time: games were played in the afternoon, and divided into periods controlled and enforced by a referee. Cricket offers a particularly interesting example of how this discourse of mechanized time was made commensurate with both competition and a style of disinterestedness. Public school cricket adhered to the regulation of time (in the last game of cricket in Tom Brown's schooldays, the game runs out of time), but batsman could play in a style which was both attentive to the rhythms of the game (for instance, by taking risks and quickening the pace of scoring), but also as if they were batting 'out of time' – as if trying too hard to score, or by playing ungainly shots, was not the right form.

There are many other manifestations of this discursive disjunction. A modern game of football runs for an allocated time (90 minutes, with extra time for injuries and in a knockout competition where scores are level at full time), while folk football usually continued until it was too dark to follow what was happening. The winner of a game of association football is determined by whichever team had scored the most goals at the completion of time, with a goal being defined quite specifically (the propelling of the ball by designated parts of the body fully across the straight marked line running between the two goalposts). With folk football the question of what constituted a score, or how winning was determined, varied from one location to another, and was something that was remembered and passed down, rather than formally recorded, defined or prescribed. In modern football a referee interprets and oversees the application of the rules, and there is a rationale, almost an economic calculation, behind the penalties handed out (handling the ball to prevent a goal, or fouling a player through on goal, will result in that player being dismissed); in folk football violence was constant, and only punished through reciprocal violence.

This sense of calculation extends to issues of fairness and equality. In modern football, teams must have the same number of players (11), and if a player was forced to leave the field because of particularly violent play, the perpetrator could be dismissed, thus evening things up; more recently, the likelihood of inequalities brought about by injury has been further addressed by the provision of substitutes. With folk football, numbers were by and large both arbitrary and changeable; things might start out with some sense of balance (one village having roughly the same number of participants as their opponents; the number of married men being roughly equal to unmarried men), but there was no imperative or rule with regard to equality.

In public school sport the space of play retained some vestige of its folk roots in that it was primarily designed for and organized in terms of participation. Some bigger grounds had a pavilion or put up tents, an obvious sign and accommodation of the spectator and spectatorship, but these were not meant for large numbers, and had a predominantly social function. At the same time, pavilions clearly facilitated some practices and rituals of spectatorship: they provided wider views of the field; they offered protection from the weather; and they allowed and even encouraged partisans of different teams to meet, sit, talk, barrack and even sing together, and to interact with and direct comments to supporters of the other team. Most of the spectators at public school football games, however, would have been located on the sidelines, separated from the participants by a piece of rope or just a white chalk line drawn on the grass. It was here that the continuity and discontinuity between folk and public school football was written in the one space; this organizational logic signalled both a proxemics (the community was in play, in the sense that spectators identified with, simulated and demonstrated a commitment to the style, form and ethos of the team and the sport) and a distancing (the team stood in for, and was spatially set apart from, the community). This scenario was not the same, of course, across all sports; the style and intensity of the participant–spectator relation being particularly idiosyncratic, for instance, in cricket. In general, however, we can suggest that the space of public school sport articulated and facilitated socio-cultural identification, in a manner that was much more intense, formalized and categorical than was the case with folk football.

We could characterize these differences as sets of discursive statements that follow from and manifest two different discursive formations, one corresponding to play, the other to the modern field of sport. These are not the only examples of the disjunction that arises in the colonization of play by sport, but they are the most significant and cogent in demonstrating the antithetical and incommensurate nature of the relation between them. At the same time we know that this parting of ways, or as John Hargreaves (1987) might have it the theft of folk games by organized sport, produced a metadiscourse whereby the field of sport traced its origins back to, and articulated a connection with, the chaotic, irrational and completely wasteful – that is to say, 'authentic' – activity of folk games-as-play. Sport, as an increasingly pervasive and institutionally valorized (by the fields of government, journalism, religion and education) discursive regime, helped transform the violent melees of folk football into relatively restrained and ordered affairs, thus reducing the instances of injury and death. More importantly it refigured these activities as sites of socio-cultural reproduction, emphasizing the value of team work, competition, self-discipline and control: feelings, passions, disaffections and emotions were to be dissipated, at a participatory and spectator level, within the confined and (more or less) safe spaces of the field and the grandstand.

The development of character

How did games-as-sport fit into this scenario, and why did the public schools privilege physical team sports such as football and cricket? Unlike Greek athletics, the Renaissance courtly tradition of formal and technical exercise, or German and Swedish gymnastics, football and cricket clearly were not vehicles for what were widely considered to be the effete pursuits of physical beauty, the harmonious configuration of body and spirit, or intellectual refinement; moreover, they required no master or overseer. Their primary function was to develop a form of character, broadly understood as an amalgam of self-reliance, loyalty, endurance, teamwork and self-sacrifice.

This experience of team sport supposedly equipped boys with a set of transferable skills and strengths that could be applied to important socio-political spheres such as government, business and colonial administration. At one level this was explicable in terms of the fairly conventional notion of the body being trained to endure and overcome physical and psychological stress and pain for the greater benefit of the team. This neatly encapsulated the apparent contradiction that public school sport developed leadership by fostering a culture of self-abnegation: the leader was not so much an individual who dominated others, but rather an exemplar who worked for and submitted his own interests to those of the team. Victorian leaders best embodied and practised the strengths and virtues of the dominant class factions (that stood in for the community), and thereby taught and propagated what it meant to be British or English. However, on another level it also provided these leaders-in-waiting with a set of durable beliefs, dispositions, attitudes and a habitus that served as a marker of socio-cultural distinction and reinforced, valorized and justified power differentials at the level of class, race and gender.

Boys would leave a public school secure in the belief that they were English gentlemen, and that there was a necessary articulation between that identity and moral, physical and cultural superiority – and further down the track, military, social, political and economic success. Immersion in this culture generated a series of performances that were strictly scripted and choreographed, and it was an article of belief that the world would follow suit. If events did not go according to plan, it was imperative that the subject should maintain the correct form in the face of adversity, defeat or worse. This partly accounts for the strong anti-intellectual culture in Public Schools: determination, action, strength and endurance defined masculinity, while boys were taught that 'most material forms of intelligence were slightly effeminate' (Mangan 1981: 106).

Discipline, surveillance and normalization

From the 1850s 'games were purposely and deliberately assimilated into the formal curriculum of the public schools: suitable facilities were constructed, headmasters insisted on pupil involvement, staff participation was increasingly expected and the creation of a legitimate rhetoric began' (Mangan 1981: 16). Their role was not just pedagogical, but also disciplinary in the sense that they served as the privileged site of surveillance and normalization. For Foucault the relation between discipline, surveillance and normalization constitutes an overlapping continuum. Discipline can be defined as the process whereby 'an individual body is moulded through an intense regime of training and surveillance into a docile subject' (Schirato et al. 2012: 80), the objective being to bring about a habitus and pattern of practice that is compliant, attentive, reliable and productive. Discipline for Foucault is intensely pedagogical, and the work that power performs, and the training it provides, is 'predicated upon, imbricated with and facilitated by various bodies of authorized knowledge' (Schirato et al. 2012: xxv). This knowledge takes many forms, although Foucault has emphasized the centrality of the role of the human sciences (psychiatry, sociology, anthropology) and cognate disciplines (architecture, geography, history). The most obvious example of the power–knowledge nexus, as it was played out in 1850s public school sport, can be found in the utilization of educational, medical, scientific and health related discourses as justifications for or explanations of the value of sport; however, these were complemented by discourses associated with or derived from philosophy, ethics, religion, classics and aesthetics. In his discussion of Hely Hutchinson Almond's tenure and philosophy as headmaster of Loretto for the period 1862–1903, J. A. Mangan points out how he blended the influence of contemporary figures such as Herbert Spencer, Charles Kingsley, Archibald MacLaren and John Ruskin:

> into a conceptual and practical whole which went under the name of 'Lorettonianism' . . . It constituted an elaborate and systematic programme of health education covering food, clothes, physical exercise, sleep, fresh air and cold baths . . . he cherished those educational ideals associated with the games field which came to distinguish the more normal public schools. He endorsed, preached and publicised the simple creed: I believe in games for the training of a boy's character. (1981: 54–5)

Mangan writes that Almond 'represents a distinctive strand in the spreading web of athleticism in the nineteenth century public school' (58), embodying 'normal as well as deviant elements of athleticism' (57). However, the culture he introduced and presided over was certainly representative in terms of its educational, ethical and scientifically supported philosophy that emphasized the relation between the playing of (some) sports as being requisite for the production of men of character. This notion of character could be identified, across the public school system, in a variety of ways, such as a respect for authority, manifested by not questioning an officials decision or integrity; a willingness to sacrifice oneself and one's own interests for the good of the team or group; self-control and clear thinking under duress; the maintenance of a sense of humour under adverse conditions; a confidence, ease and assurance in dealing with others; a highly developed work ethic; and most of all by an adherence to the values and ethos of devoting oneself to the good of the team.

Athletics and bio-power

Discipline was tied in with processes of surveillance: in school, but most particularly on the playing field, boys were subject to three specific forms of gaze, all of which were concerned with the identification and repeated confirmation of signs of character. The first of these emanated from the masters, the second from one's schoolmates, and the third was the student's gaze turned back upon the self. All three were central to the student's attaining and maintaining the status of a legitimate subject within the networks of power that existed both within and beyond the physical boundaries of the school.

The set of physical activities gathered together within and as the newly instituted field of sport, and the networks of surveillance that accompanied them, constituted an elaborate system of bio-power: they became a way of seeing, experiencing and understanding the world and the self; worked to produce naturalized dispositions-as-subjects; served as a set of templates against which subjects measured their 'non-coincidence' with themselves; and finally described 'the dispersion of subjects', measuring 'the interstices' that separated them and the 'distances . . . between them' (Foucault 1998: 313). Practices of differentiation between the healthy and the sick, the vigorous and the lazy, and the normal and the deviant were processed and organized through sport-as-discourse. The discourses and practices of sport were particularly useful in this regard because they carried out the imperatives of bio-power in an economical way: through sport the body was simultaneously exercised, disciplined, educated, disposed and diverted.

Foucault argues that from the eighteenth century the deployment of the technologies and discourses of discipline, surveillance and normalization, in sites such as barracks, prisons, the workplace and schools, was part of 'an increasingly controlled, more rational, and economic process of adjustment' that had been sought 'between productive activities, communication networks, and the play of power relations' (2001: 339). These techniques and discourses were initially applied to the wider population-as-resource, but Hargreaves argues that public schools took the various apparatuses and techniques of surveillance that were employed to monitor and discipline the populace and deployed them 'for the first time, on the sons of the dominant classes themselves' (1987: 42). He writes that:

> In the public schools a new disciplinary technology was discovered and developed . . . Like the workhouses, asylums, hospitals, prisons, barracks and factories of the era, these schools closed off the individual from society, subjecting him to the uninterrupted gaze of authority. Young adolescent males were 'normalized' by subjecting them to detailed, minute, continuous, comprehensive surveillance in Spartan conditions. Unlike these other institutions, however, what was unique about the public schools was their discovery, development and deployment of the new athleticist technology . . . putting it in more conventional terms, the idea that a moral education could be imparted through games, and what they thereby imparted, was their one original contribution to 'educational theory' and practice. Athleticist discourse, the knowledge

produced in athleticist practices, and the techniques that were developed, represented an entirely new disciplinary strategy: by extending the gaze of authority beyond work and rest into the world of play, the body was made uninterruptedly visible and control was thereby extended over the 'soul' of the individual (the 'character' in athleticist discourse). (42)

Askesis and agonistics

Athletics and athleticist technologies and discourses, which constituted the apparatus of an ethical and moral training-as-normalization, were at least partly derived from the wider and influential discursive form of Victorian Hellenism (Adams 2006; Hughson 2009; Jenkyns 1980). The manner in which this Hellenistic legacy inflected athletics in public schools can be divided into two main forms: the first, and dominant mode, was informed by the Greek notions of *askesis* and agonistics, and was also closely associated with Victorian 'muscular Christianity'; the second mode, largely identified with the intellectual work of Pater, Ruskin and Mathew Arnold, had a strong aesthetic element.

Foucault argues (2005) that in Classical Greece *askesis* was tied to the disposition to take care of the self, and involves and requires constant self-interrogation, testing and training. The idea was that just as a successful athlete must constantly train and exercise in order to overcome personal limitations, so any citizen wishing to participate in and contribute to public life must be in the right shape, figuratively speaking. He suggests that the principles and techniques of the care of the self were relatively constant and homogeneous in Classical Greece, although allowances would need to be made for context-specific variations and different forms of emphasis. This situation changes, to some extent, in the Hellenistic and Roman periods. The procedures and techniques of *askesis* were 'considerably amplified', were subject to increased codification, organization and categorization, and became a 'subject matter for teaching and constituted one of the basic instruments used in the direction of souls' (Foucault 1986b: 74). Foucault provides the following, more general account of the changes, from which Christianity was to 'borrow extensively':

A mistrust of the pleasures, an emphasis on the consequences of their abuse for the body and the soul, a valorization of marriage and marital obligations, a disaffection with regard to the spiritual meanings imputed to the love of boys: a whole attitude of severity was manifested in the thinking of philosophers and physicians in the course of the first two centuries . . . More precisely, there was a greater apprehension concerning the sexual pleasures, more attention given to the relation that one might have with them. (39)

For Foucault these regimes of *askesis* were increasingly oriented towards the production of knowledge that would facilitate a discovery of the truth of the self. The exercises, self-examinations and self-preparations of the Cynics and related schools of philosophy of this period effect a 'double decoupling' of the relationship between *askesis* and self-knowledge that previously characterized Platonic and Neoplatonic thought (Foucault 2005: 420). The first part of this process removes self-knowledge from 'the central axis of the *askesis*' (420): its place is now occupied by the precepts that allow the subject to deal with and overcome (or at least remain unmoved with regard to) the vicissitudes of everyday life, in much the same way that a well-prepared athlete is able to meet all the challenges of a contest (322). The second change involves a shift away from the notion that self-knowledge is derived from recognition of the divine within oneself. Foucault suggests this double 'decoupling' of *askesis* and self-knowledge, and self-knowledge and the divine 'was at the source of the historical success of these exercises, of their historical success, paradoxically, in Christianity itself' (420).

Foucault insists that this break does not produce anything that could be mistaken for the Christian version of *askesis*; but it does anticipate and facilitate it. He demonstrates this by way of reference to the trope of the athlete as it functions in the two orders of discourse. In Stoic thought the athlete is to be differentiated from other practitioners of physical exercise, such as the dancer. Whereas the dancer works towards embodying a certain ideal that requires surpassing or leaving the self behind, the activities, thoughts and the bodily hexis of the wrestler in competition is always attuned to the relation between the intersection of the self and the moment. The Christian athlete, on the other hand, is in some ways like the dancer, in that they are:

> on the indefinite path of progress towards holiness in which he must surpass himself even to the point of renouncing himself. Also, the Christian athlete is especially someone who has an enemy . . . who keeps him on guard. With regard to whom and to what? But with regard to himself! To himself, inasmuch as the most malign and dangerous powers he has to confront (sin, fallen nature, seduction by the devil, etcetera) are within himself. The Stoic athlete . . . has to be ready for a struggle in which his adversary is . . . coming to him from the external world . . . The ancient athlete is an athlete of the event. The Christian is an athlete of himself. (322)

The two main point of connection between these otherwise quite different regimes is that, first, Christianity inherits what Foucault terms 'the old Stoic suspicion towards oneself' (422); and second, Christianity takes on and develops the important role accorded to the master and guide in Stoic thought and activity. The ascetic exercises of the Stoic athlete were to proliferate under Christianity: manuals of exercises, devotions and procedures and regimes of abstinence and sacrifice, all woven into the fabric of the subject's daily life, from morning to night, and from birth to death; prescribed and specified in terms of quantity, temporality and intensity; and inscribed with a direction, a function, a narrative of utility. The Christian athlete (who in time becomes a soldier) will be even better prepared than the Stoic, being equipped with the extra advantage of a much more imposing and authoritative corpus of texts, rules and techniques; the Christian adheres to, lives out and manifests the rules (the word of God) that lead to salvation. Moreover, this path to salvation is not only signposted everywhere and everyday; there is also a variety of institutionally authorized guides to advise, support, encourage and, where necessary, rebuke. This is perhaps where Christianity departs most radically from the ethos and practices of the care of the self that characterize Classical Greece. As Foucault writes:

> From the moment that the culture of the self was taken up by Christianity, it was . . . put to work for the exercise of . . . pastoral power . . . insofar as individual salvation is channelled – to a certain extent, at least – through a pastoral institution that has the care of the soul as its object, the classical care of the self disappeared, that is, was integrated and lost a large part of its autonomy. (1997: 278)

In Victorian public schools a version of *askesis* was augmented and extended by being tied in with the notion of agonistics, which can be translated as the taking part in a contest or competition (Vernant and Vidal-Naquet 1990: 249). As Richard Jenkyns writes, the Victorian age:

> was intensely competitive; the industrial revolution had broken down the exclusive predominance of the old landed aristocracy, and enabled men as never before to fight their way from comparative obscurity to positions of wealth and power. The spirit of competition spilled over into the schools and the universities, where foreign observers were struck by the English passion for competitive sports. (1980: 215)

The imperative to compete also manifested itself as a form of *askesis*: competition was, at a discursive level, never simply played out with and against the other, but with regard to the overcoming of the weaknesses, fears and limitations of the self. This was reflected in the concomitant discourse about the ethical superiority of competing as against trying too hard and making victory an end in itself; although here the question of aristocratic form and style, of an ease and confidence with regard to the world and one's place in it, and one's superiority with regard to other classes, are also significant features. The discursive significance of agonistics-as-*askesis* can be seen in the unspoken prohibition, in school cricket games, against taking pleasure in beating or running up a score against an inferior opponent. In neither case did the action demand or prove anything with regard to the self; it facilitated winning, but indicated nothing more than a willingness to take advantage of the limitations of others.

The self-overcoming that is honed and demonstrated within competitive sport is, simultaneously, a form of self-effacement. The limitations of the self are surpassed not so as to facilitate self-aggrandizement or the attainment of personal glory. Rather, the individual attains a form of (normative) subjectivity, becomes one of us, precisely in his disappearance: weaknesses of body (tiredness, a lack of speed) and mind (fear, stress, doubts) give way to the superior call of duty, of sacrificing the self for the good of the team. In *Tom Brown's School-Days*, Tom's first moment of recognition within the school, on the part of both boys and the masters, is when he throws his body under the opposition's charge, helps protect the ball, and so earns right to be spoken of 'Who is he?' (Hughes 1974: 109). On one of his last days at Rugby, the following exchange takes place, at a cricket match, between Tom, his friend Arthur, and one of the masters:

'I'm beginning to understand the game scientifically. What a noble game it is, too!'

'Isn't it? But it's more than a game. It's an institution', said Tom.

'Yes', said Arthur, 'the birthright of British boys old and young, as *habeas corpus* and trial by jury are of British men.'

'The discipline and reliance on one another which it teaches is so valuable, I think', went on the master, 'it ought to be such an unselfish game. It merges the individual in the eleven; he doesn't play that he may win, but that his side may.'

'That's very true,' said Tom, 'and that's why football and cricket . . . are such much better games than fives or hare-and-hounds, or any others where the object is to come in first or to win for one's self, and not that one's side may win.' (300)

As Rugby inches closer to a victory over the team from Lords, the game is interrupted by the arrival of the omnibus that is to take the visitors back to town. Stumps are drawn and the Lords team wins on a technicality, but:

such a defeat is a victory. So think Tom and all the School eleven, as they accompany their conquerors to the omnibus, and send them off with three ringing cheers, after Mr. Aislabie has shaken hands all round, saying to Tom, 'I must compliment you, sir, on your eleven, and I hope we shall have you for a member if you come up to town.' (303)

While the 'other side' of Victorian Hellenism emphasized beauty, balance, sensitivity and intellectual refinement, values that did not figure prominently in the culture of public school sport, it retained an interest in and admiration for the notion of *askesis*, and came to see the school athlete as an embodiment of Greek ideals. The key figures here are Walter Pater, Charles Kingsley and Mathew Arnold. Pater had a strong attachment to *askesis*, and repeatedly drew 'analogies between Spartan training and a Victorian public school education' (Allen 2006: 230); this analogy between the Spartans and the ethos of Victorian public school sport was predicated upon self-sacrifice and team spirit, of youth committing themselves 'absolutely, soul and body, to a corporate sentiment' (Jenkyns 1980: 223). Pater thought that Greek statues, particularly statues of athletes, showed 'forms of men and women whose every limb and attitude betokened perfect health, and grace, and power, and a self-possession and self-restraint so habitual and complete that it had become unconscious' (Allen 2006: 218). For both Pater and Kingsley, the body of the public school Christian gentleman was 'the incarnation of *askesis*, a discipline at once physical and intellectual' (216); and 'the heroic athletes of Greek art' were 'superbly reincarnated as cricketers on the banks of the Thames' (231).

Arnold brought a more critical eye to, and an awareness of, the intellectual limitations of public school athletics. Hellenism provided 'the indispensible basis of conduct and self-control' (Arnold 1979: 136), but the Victorian 'passion for field sports . . . for the body and for all manly exercise' (103) was part of a barbarian aristocratic culture that was:

> an exterior culture mainly. It consisted principally in outward gifts and graces, in looks, manners, accomplishments, prowess . . . Far within, and unawakened, lay a whole range of powers of thought and feeling, to which these interesting productions of nature had, from the circumstances of their life, no access. (103)

Arnold's characterization of public school athleticism as essentially a style of being, rather than an embodiment of Hellenistic virtues, was reflected in the strong anti-intellectualism that developed in Victorian public schools, and which came to be associated with sport. What is also useful to note here is the association of school sport, and by extension its style, form and ethos, with a specific class faction – the aristocracy, and to some extent the upper-middle-class faction that aspired to join them. Bourdieu points out that this linkage – between the sporting ethos, anti-intellectualism and class politics – constitutes one of the more significant legacies that the contemporary socio-cultural derives from public schools:

> Glorification of sport as the training ground of character . . . always implies a certain anti-intellectualism. When one remembers that the dominant faction of the dominant class always tends to conceive their relation to the dominated faction – 'intellectuals', 'artists', 'professors' – in terms of the opposition between the male and the female, the virile

and the effeminate, which is given different contents depending on the period . . . one understands one of the most important implications of the exaltation of sport and especially of 'manly' sports like rugby, and it can be seen that sport . . . is an object of struggles between the fractions of the dominant class and also between social classes. (Bourdieu 1991: 361)

Athletics as cultural form

We can consider this relationship between team games, the notion of a sporting ethos and the pedagogical process that produces the relevant habitus, by way of an analysis of the game of cricket as it was played in English public schools of the mid-nineteenth century (and to some extent today). Theoretically, players were simply taking part in a physical activity defined and delimited by a codified set of rules; but if that is all they were doing, it certainly was not cricket. The saying 'it isn't cricket', which passed into the wider socio-cultural field as an indicator of a mode of behaviour that is (ethically or morally) unacceptable, is predicated on an understanding and acceptance of the notion of fair play, which is a very different thing from an adherence to rules. To give some examples, if a player bowls a ball and the person batting gets an edge that is not detected by the umpire, the correct thing for the batter to do is to 'walk'. Similarly, if an umpire rules incorrectly that a fielder has caught a hit on the full, the fielder should automatically own up to the fact that the catch was not taken.

In most cases the fact that someone is playing cricket means they have to be treated as if they are adherents to the ethos of fair play. In other words, it isn't cricket to act as if or suggest that what the opposition is doing isn't cricket: if you believe in the ethos, then you have to believe in its more or less ineluctable efficacy. So if a person batting hits the ball and the umpire is unsure whether the catch has been taken, the correct form is for the batter to ask of the fielder, by as unobtrusive a means as possible (say, a raising of the head as half-posed question), if the ball was caught; for the fielder to nod; and for the batter to immediately and undemonstratively accept this by walking off. What we are dealing with here is not so much a set of practices that accord with playing fairly (you don't cheat), but rather the notion of fair play as pure style. Players were required to demonstrate, in an unobtrusive and natural manner, that winning was not the most important consideration – regardless of how important the game was.

The reluctance on the part of cricket players to take advantage of these strategies and techniques shows the extent to which the public school sports ethos functioned simultaneously as a form of distinction and discipline. Seeming to do everything in an effortless, confident, assured and disinterested manner were markers that distinguished the upper from the lower classes, and naturalized the power differentials that separated them. When labourers or mechanics played sport, they not only tried too hard – they looked like they were trying. Their ultra-competitive, utility-driven behaviour was translated as a cynical disregard for the spirit of the game, and just another manifestation of their selfishness and lack of any kind of a civilizing influence, which by extension valorized the exclusion of their class from decision-making apparatuses. As long as this notion of the value of team work and embodied disinterestedness permeated the socio-cultural as a kind of productive and taken-for-granted truth, it spoke to both the upper and the lower classes, reinforcing the superiority–inferiority binary that defined and determined everything about the way they related to each other. And the message to the middle class was equally clear: public schools, and the team games they played, taught your sons to fit, as seamlessly as possible, into the world of the dominant class.

Conclusion

The propagation of this sporting ethos within public schools was clearly part of a configuration of discourses – albeit a particularly privileged one – that generated and rationalized social, cultural, political and economic practices in Victorian England. Public schools and their games culture were central to the way the civilizing (and more broadly, nationalizing and imperializing) processes was played out, despite the relatively small percentage of the population who had direct experience of it, to the extent that by the end of the Victorian period, sport and the notion of fair play was (almost universally) synonymous with British national character. One of the reasons for this was that the value accorded to teamwork, whether at the level of competitive games or politics. That the Victorian public school ethos and discourses of sport were successfully transplanted both to the wider field of sport, including the working classes, and to its imperial and eventually global extensions, testifies to its efficacy as a pedagogical, disciplinary and normative apparatus. As Bourdieu writes:

> In reality, the development of sporting activity itself, even among working class youngsters, doubtlessly results partly from the fact that sport was predisposed to fulfil, on a much larger scale, the very same functions which underlay its invention in the late nineteenth century English public schools. Even before they saw sport as a means of 'improving character' in accordance with Victorian belief, the public schools . . . which have to carry out their supervisory task twenty four hours a day, seven days a week, saw sport as 'a means of filling in time', an economical way of occupying the adolescents who were their full-time responsibility.

When the pupils are on the sports field, they are easy to supervise, they are engaged in healthy activity and they are venting their violence on each other rather than destroying the buildings or shouting down their teachers; that is why . . . 'organized sport will last as long as the public schools'. (1991: 365)

The discursive legacy that the Public Schools passed on to Victorian and Edwardian British culture proved to be both highly durable, but also susceptible to change, and even transformation. Public school sport may have functioned as a site for the training of Victorian elites, but it was taken up and popularized, and used for their own ends and purposes, both by the middle and lower classes in Britain, by British colonies, and by disaffected nationalist who had no commitment to the British Empire. In our next chapters we will give an account of how these changes inflected and to some extent transformed the field of sport.

CHAPTER FOUR

Victorian sport

Introduction

In his account of his last Antarctic expedition, Captain Robert Falcon Scott (2012) repeatedly refers to how in the midwinter of 1911, when all exploratory and much scientific work was suspended due to the severe weather conditions and the lack of light, the men went outside most days to play football; the only other activity observed on a comparably regular basis was the Sunday Service. Scott does not make much of this or dwell on details: he occasionally mentions which players were the best footballers, that the exercise was good for them and helped keep them warm, and that the game was a means of maintaining *esprit de corps* and morale among the men; but there is no wider justification or explanation as to why football was played consistently, particularly in such extreme conditions.

Scott's final expedition took place just before the First World War, at a time when the legacy of Victorian Britain's presumptions, values and discourses still held sway, and the modern field of sport, the establishment of which John Hargraves refers to as 'a major cultural achievement of the mid-Victorian period' (1987: 45), had taken on a hegemonic role within British culture. Consequently there was really no need to make a case for the usefulness or place of sport, even in conditions that militated against it, or occasionally rendered it as a travesty of the real thing. For Scott, Antarctic football was an important site for the maintenance of the 'between us' of the group, even as it doubtlessly degenerated into something both farcical and difficult to endure. In this context it resembles what Slavoj Zizek calls an ideological *sinthome* (1991: 129), which he defines as the formulaic repetition of a non-sensical cultural form (a song, a game) that facilitates social bonding and/as 'idiotic enjoyment' (129). This form of idiotic enjoyment, developed in and initially exclusive to elitist English public schools, eventually colonized Victorian England and much of the British Empire, and by the beginning of the twentieth century was well on its way to establishing itself as a global, rather than merely a British, cultural form and discourse.

Sport and modernity

Victorian sport was strongly inflected by public school athletics, with its emphasis on fair play, teamwork, participation, competition and self-overcoming. However, towards the end of the Victorian period athletics had been taken up by entirely new and wider demographics, and had become a more bureaucratized, standardized and codified set of activities, with a strong spectator and commercial focus. One of the most significant factors in bringing about this development was what Guttmann (1978) refers to as the set of discourses and technologies of modernization. He argues that characteristics associated with modernization, such as secularism, democracy and equality, specialization, rationalization, bureaucratization and quantification, were influential in the rise of national and international governing bodies (such as the AAA, the FA, the IOC and FIFA); brought about the standardization of rules, team numbers, distances and dimensions (of playing fields and equipment), and the concept of the records; and facilitated the extension of support services and roles, such managers, physios, psychologists, skills coaches and staff with scientific, sports medicine and dietary expertise.

In the Victorian period, sport developed along lines derived from distinctively rationalist imperatives. In the second part of the nineteenth century, sport became the microcosmic version of the macrocosmic modern state with its productive and transformative bureaucratic apparatuses, discourses and specialized roles (Guttmann 1978). The scale and complexity of sporting apparatuses and organizations increased as:

> ruling bodies emerged at the centre to co-ordinate individual sports, adjudicate disputes and formulate policy. New playing techniques were invented and developed and new types of equipment came into use. Roles in sport, both playing and administrative, became more specialized. These sports became less like gladiatorial contests and more like scientific exercises in improvement – matters of safer, measured, exact, ordered achievement. Controlling bodies were formed for a number of major sports to co-ordinate the activity of the many sports clubs of different kinds that had sprung up all over the country – the Football Association (FA) in 1863, the Amateur Athletic Club in 1866, the Amateur Swimming Association in 1869 . . . Major competitions were inaugurated – the FA Cup (1971), the Amateur, Professional and Open Golf Championships

(1858–61), the Oxford and Cambridge Boat Race (1849) . . . And new major organized sports like tennis, gymnastics, croquet, bicycling and mountain climbing, caught on rapidly. (Hargreaves 1987: 45)

Neil Tranter (1992) has disputed both the extent of the codification of sport in the Victorian period, and the assumption that all sports benefited from or were carried along by this development. He makes the point that governing bodies, with the power to institute and modify rules and conditions of membership, were already established in several prominent sports (cricket, golf, horseracing) in the eighteenth century; that in some regions of Britain the standardization and codification of sports, and the establishment of regular competitions, was not achieved until the Edwardian period; and that certain sports (professional rowing and athletics, the Scottish game of shinty) went into near-terminal decline during the second half of the nineteenth century (14–15). However he acknowledges that:

> the fundamental characteristics of late Victorian and Edwardian sport were very different from those of the early Victorian period. in less than fifty years the number of sports and the numbers playing and watching increased dramatically, the social composition of participants and the spatial parameters of the sports they practiced substantially widened, codification, institutionalisation, commercialism and professionalism became widespread for the first time, and the timing of sporting activity radically altered . . . Sport, in its modern, organised, commercialised and extensive form, was truly an 'invention' of the Victorian and Edwardian age. (15–16)

This emphasis on the role of the discursive production of Victorian sport is not meant to downplay the significance of the quite dramatic changes in material conditions and contexts that occurred in the nineteenth century (industrialization, urbanization, transport, new communication technologies and Empire); clearly they facilitated the rise and spread of modern field of sport. However, material conditions are always the products of, or at least imbricated with, discursive regimes. As Armand Mattelart has demonstrated, an apparently autonomous technological development such as the 'internationalization of communications was spawned by two forms of universalism: the Enlightenment and liberalism' (2000: 1). Liberalism itself, along with its various imperatives relating to the free circulation of goods, services, peoples, texts and ideas arose as a response to and critique of the various interventions (economic, social, political) of government and the reason of state in the lives and affairs of its citizens (Foucault 1997: 75). The civilizing process, imperialism, nationalism, liberalism and capitalism colonized games (such as cricket and football), to the extent that they helped produce not just the objectivities of the modern field of sport (institutions, specific games, rules, fixture lists, national competitions), but an entirely new set of embodied practices, dispositions and values – what Bourdieu (1991) calls the field of sport and its specific habitus.

Sporting missionaries

The process whereby sport, as both a set of formalized and rationalized practices and a discursive ethos, was taken up across class, political and ethnic categories and demographics has been partly explained by factors such as improvements in transport and communications (Hargreaves 1987; Holt 1989; Mangan 2002); the rise of industrialized cities in the north of Britain and the spread of urbanization (Guttmann 1978); an increase in leisure time (Brailsford 1991); and the desire of the middle classes to emulate the cultural activities of the upper classes (Bourdieu 1991). However, the dissemination and popularization of sport-as-ethos, and by extension the establishment of sport as an autonomous and coherent cultural field, can be traced to the trajectories and activities of the graduates of Victorian public schools. As Mangan writes:

> the late nineteenth and early twentieth centuries were marvellous moments for athletically-inclined educationalists who became influential arbiters of orthodoxy . . . teachers . . . defined moral conduct and conveyed those doctrines which 'impinged on faith and practice' and which were considered fundamental for the requirements of middle-class life. The universities provided continuity and stability for a 'flow of masters' to the schools which then reproduced a 'systematic body of doctrine' which then perpetrated a way of life. (2002: 4)

The symbiotic relation between public school and university athletics ensured that this increasingly systematized 'extensive and common practice of "play" was eventually put in place across the world' (3). However, the initial point of development was not the elementary schools, which originally favoured drill, and only introduced sports into school curriculum during the Edwardian period (83); instead sporting clubs sprang up among the populous industrial centres such as Birmingham and Manchester. From the 1880s organized sport managed to become, in Hargreaves' terms, 'the basis of the dominant class's hegemony' (1987: 57–8) over the increasingly visible and politically active working class. Class disaffection and hostility, widespread poverty, the social dislocation that was a significant consequence of the growth of industrial cities, youth delinquency, the agitations of the suffragette movement and the perception that the nations moral and physical health was in a state of decline combined to produce 'the threat of instability' and a sense among the dominant classes of 'A widespread sense of an impending clash at home' (57). This gave rise to a:

> sustained and variegated attempt . . . by a section of the dominant class to adapt, extend and deploy athleticist technology as part of a programme of class conciliation and control, using a 'philanthropic strategy'. To the sports-oriented missionizing institutions of the mid-Victorian era already implicated in this emergent programme – the Volunteers, the working men's clubs, the local political clubs, the Young Men's Christian association . . . the Sunday Schools and other socio-religious organizations were now added a series of missionizing movements, agencies and their attendant discourses . . . One clear indication of the churches' involvement in the deployment of sport as part of this kind of enterprise is their success in promoting football. A quarter of Birmingham's teams were church-connected in 1880, and in Liverpool in 1900 local teams originated almost exclusively from church organizations. A significant proportion of the clubs which later formed the core of the Football League were sponsored by socio-religious bodies – among them Bolton, Wolverhampton Wanderers, Aston Villa, Birmingham City, Swindon, and Tottenham Hotspur. (Hargreaves 1987: 58–9)

Sporting missionaries used the lure of play-as-sport as a normative facility, much as was the case in public schools, although the disciplining of male working-class bodies and minds was not oriented towards preparing them for leadership or inculcating a sense and style of superiority. It served, instead, as a substitute for various forms of socio-cultural violence, mitigated the effects of alcohol consumption, and normalized a conformity and submission with regard to social conventions, rules and figures of authority. This 'expansion of reconstructed sports' (45) helped individual sports to organize and reproduce themselves, facilitated their incorporation into national and eventually international bodies, and produced many new sites for, and methods of, involving individuals, local communities and national groups.

The extent and rapidity of the expansion of sport-as-field, not to mention as a form of popular entertainment and paid employment, was hardly envisaged or welcomed by the ex-public school boys who became colonial administrators, civil servants, lawyers, academics, clergymen, school teachers, bankers and businessmen, and who founded, defined and codified most of the significant sports organizations and competitions of the time. In fact, prior to the 1870s many sports were doing everything they could to limit participation to the 'right types': for instance, 'the Amateur Athletic Club, founded in 1866 by Oxford and Cambridge men . . . was to exclude not only those who had competed in races for money but all manual workers' (Holt 1989: 108); the Amateur Rowing Association did their best to keep out mechanics, 'all those who had to work with their hands for a living' (108), international crews tainted by professional connections, and even engineers (Birley 1995: 59); and the inclination of educated, middle-class women to take up recreational cycling was considered particularly scandalous.

From athletics to popular sport

While the discourses of public school athletics were not congruent with popularization, nor with commercial logics and relationships, sport in its incipient forms in the eighteenth and early nineteenth centuries had found itself caught up in what Frow has characterized, more generally, as:

> the struggle that is waged, perhaps particularly in advanced capitalist societies, over the line of demarcation between what can be properly bought and sold and what cannot. Every society withdraws certain domains from market relations. The domain of religion, of personal life . . . the political sphere, the sphere of public services, that of art and some kinds of writing may conform, or may be presumed to conform, to a different logic from that of strict profit maximization. Exchanges in these spheres are not governed by the market; while things and services may be alienable in the sense of being transferable from one person or group to another, they are nevertheless . . . market-inalienable. (1997: 131)

Cricket and horseracing are examples of sports that were dominated by social elites and socio-cultural rather than economic capital (at least at the level of controlling bodies such as the MCC and the Jockey Club), but which were also characterized by professionalism and subsidized by high levels of gambling. While membership of clubs and controlling bodies was highly exclusive and dependant upon social status, at the same time the need to employ professionals meant that economic considerations were an everyday, practical reality.

For a time, football resisted commercialism. The Football Association was formed in 1863, and it introduced a body of rules that was accepted in Britain in 1882 (Mason 1980: 15–16). The FA was initially dominated by officials such as Charles Alcock, a old Harrovian who served as secretary for 25 years and set up the FA Cup on the model of a Harrow house competition (Mason 1980: 16). Until the 1880s, amateurism and athleticism remained the dominant mode and discourse, fixtures were largely informal and regionally based, and southern clubs dominated the only nation wide competition, the FA Cup:

> When London clubs met clubs from the regions, which they were doing more often as the 1870s drew to a close, they usually won. Members of all

social classes played although the majority of players were increasingly working men. But in and around London both the Football association and the leading clubs were dominated by either leisured gentlemen or by professionally or commercially employed products of the public and grammar schools. Most of these men almost certainly subscribed to some variant of the healthy mind in the healthy body syndrome. Play was good for you but it was also done for fun. It was not to be confused with work which was also good for you. Playing for money was something gentlemen did not do. (Mason 1980: 69)

Amateurism retained a hegemonic role and status with the field, institutions and discourses of cricket; however, cricket's history of commercial spectatorship, gambling and entrepreneurial activity militated against any adoption of the same strict and exclusive policy towards professionalism that characterized rugby, rowing and athletics. Cricket was governed, from the late eighteenth century on, by an exclusivist and elitist organization (the MCC) that was strongly committed to what it saw as the symbiotic virtues of the preservation of the sporting ethos and upper-class governance. As well as presiding, in a generally conservative manner, over rules pertaining to bowling actions, the size of the follow-on and other technical matters, it maintained the distinction accorded to supposedly amateur gentlemen up to the 1960s.

Cricket may have been, as far as the English upper and middle classes were concerned, 'the citadel of true sporting values' (Birley 1995: 16), but from the entrepreneurial circuses of the eighteenth century to the time of the professional-in-all-but-name W. G. Grace it was inextricably tied in with, if publicly disdainful of, market forces and money. While it never suffered from 'the commercialism and excessive competition that afflicted football' (27), it did eventually set up a first-class county league with a fixture list and a points regime. Cricket continued to be associated with and defined by a public school style and ethos, and county cricket was never particularly businesslike nor lost its upper-class affiliations. However, the configuration of its status as the national sport and the advent of international competition meant that the MCC and county clubs were burdened with mostly well-behaved and polite crowds, popular press coverage, star status accorded to its best players, and competitive colonials who were not always white and had never graced the playing fields of Eton.

The materiality and the idea of the playing fields of Eton constituted one example of a strand of discursive statements relating to sporting space, place and architecture. We have already referred to space as one important means of distinguishing between folk and public school football; as sport was taken up by wider demographics and gradually become more of a heteronomous field, this transition was manifested spatially and architecturally. Space and architecture, like every discursive statement, are formed through, and articulate, power relations. Changes to spatial and architectural forms, relations and configurations are a sign of power in action, a reflection of the discursive formation that is hegemonic within that field; but space and architecture are also a palimpsest, a material history of what has won out and what has been superseded. Space also functions as a disciplinary and regulatory mechanism, in that it controls, shapes and inflects cultural tempos, rhythms, trajectories, meanings and stories, while simultaneously being overlaid by and carrying the traces of different discursive trajectories and formations.

The transition from public school to Victorian sport was played out in this overlaying of spatial discourses, accentuated by the moving of games from an area that was part of the institution and community, adjacent and continuous with regard to the main sites of the school (buildings, monuments, statues), to parks, stadiums or grounds that were located within and served a much wider community. The organization of materiality and space within larger stadiums constituted a significant discursive break from public school sport; unlike school grounds, they were to a large extent configured and built to fit as many people into the ground, without serious regard for questions of comfort, accessibility or visibility. Generally, football grounds were fairly primitive places, although the more successful clubs were forced to do more because of the size of their crowds:

> By 1885 the Preston ground had much in common with twentieth-century English football stadiums. Staging (terracing?) had been erected all along the ground opposite the grandstand, and at the two ends which gives the place the appearance of a huge amphitheatre. But Preston was very much a member of the football *avant garde* in the 1880s. elsewhere, terracing was by no means universal. wagonettes and other vehicles were often brought into the grounds and used as stands. On many grounds, the ordinary standing customer, especially if of modest height, must have found seeing the play a bit of a problem if the crowd was at all large. (Mason 1980: 140)

One of the consequences of this early configuration of increasingly large crowds and the makeshift space and architecture at the grounds was a democratizing or breaking down of class-inflected spatial arrangements, something that could hardly be considered or experienced in any other socio-cultural in Victorian Britain:

> In 1877 . . . the Athletic News did a feature on the Bramall Lane Ground in Sheffield. It noted that the 'immense audiences' who turned up for a 'good match' at cricket or football 'are not drawn from one class of people. Each grade of society sends its quota.' Commenting on the huge crowd at the Preston North End-Great Lever cup-tie in 1883 the Preston Herald said it was composed of 'all sorts and conditions of men, rich and poor, employers and employed'. Another northern paper emphasised the

same point five years later. 'Next to the race course a football field of the Midlands and north country presents the most hetrogenious [*sic*] mass of humanity. Rags and tatters and good old broadcloth awaited with equal impatience the beginning of the context, and in the struggle for places social inequalities were totally forgotten. (151)

The same diversity was not evident with regard to gender; very few women attended football games, although they were more likely to be seen as participants in gendered sports such as hockey and tennis; when they did attend, they were invariably middle or upper-middle class, and were usually accommodated in the pavilion (Mason 1980). Working-class women, especially those with children, were an obvious absence; they were unlikely to have the spare time to attend matches.

While Victorian sport largely maintained the temporal rhythms and patterns of public school athletics, it also gradually accommodated the imperatives of professionalized and popular sport. The most significant development involved the scheduling of sporting contests on Saturday afternoons, when workers had free time. This institutionalizing of the connection between Saturday and sport:

looked at over the broad span of the centuries, was a novelty. Its contribution to the late Victorian sporting revolution was far-reaching. The reconstructed leisure time-table, of which the free Saturday afternoon became the dominant feature, altered more than the simple timing of play. it modified the sports themselves, urging upon them a compactness and order. Saturday sport came slowly. It found its place gradually, over some forty years, varying from sport to sport and from town to town. Newly organized sports, such as football and athletics, not bound by any existing calendar ties, quickly seized upon the new free afternoon, while the older spectator sports moved more slowly, except when alert commercial interests produced a response to the customers' changed leisure time . . . It was a Bradfordian who, in the late nineteenth century, claimed that Saturday afternoon had become . . . 'as it were, part of our religion'. (Brailsford 1991: 105)

The gradual reconfiguration of sports time, and its incorporation into the logics, demands and rhythms of professionalism, spectatorship and capitalism had its equivalence at the level of the body and bodily hexis. The relation and orientation of public school athletics to the body was threefold: first, the body was a sign and a product of the control that the athlete exercised over himself; second, it showed his ease and comfort in the world, and his natural superiority over the lower classes and natives; third, it manifested the duality of his physical and moral health. The main difference that professionalism introduced was a strongly utilitarian discourse with regard to the care of the body. In football, for instance, professionals had to treat their bodies as the basis of their livelihood; they were no longer temples of moral virtue, but assets that were required to outperform their competitors on a weekly basis, in order to maximize their earning potential. Similarly, elite football teams treated their players as mechanisms, resources and commodities: consequently they introduced much more intensive and regular forms of training and preparation; provided specialized knowledge and skills (in the form of trainers and coaches); and ensured that players had access to relevant medical expertise and products (to facilitate the healing of injuries, to monitor and improve their fitness, to help make decisions about who was fit to take the field and perform).

By the mid-1880s, professional football was becoming an unspoken commonplace, with paid players being imported from outside the locality (sometimes from as far afield as Scotland, where the opposition to professionalism was particularly strong), often to help in FA Cup ties. The issue was debated fiercely before professionalism was legalized in 1885, but those who accepted money for playing had restrictions placed on their mobility (one team per season), and were not allowed to sit on FA committees or represent their club (Mason 1980). Public school affiliations, discourses and cultural capital remained dominant, however, both within controlling bodies and on the field. In 1886 in an England versus Scotland international the only professional picked for the game 'was made to wear a different shirt from the rest of the eleven' (Mason 1980: 76), and:

> in spite of their increasing lack of success against professionals, amateurs continued to find it relatively easy to get into England teams right up to 1900. And an amateur would always be appointed captain. In 1894–5, for example, the Professionals played the amateurs in an international trial at Nottingham and won 9–0. Consequently only one amateur was chosen for the England side, but he was appointed captain. (76)

The logics, discourses, values and politics that drove developments in football in the Victorian period differed from athletics, rowing, tennis and other elite-dominated amateur sports, and even from the hybrid that was cricket, because of its strong commercial affiliations. As football took a hold in northern cities, drew large crowds, and gave rise to successful teams (Blackburn Rovers, Preston North End, Bolton Wanderers), it carved out a role and a status for itself that depended out, but clearly outstripped, its initial function as a space of play and escape from the everyday.

This development was mainly played out in two related ways. First, football games became the privileged site of cultural identification, at least as far as the male population was concerned. Going to the football was not just about having fun, appreciating skill or getting caught up in an exciting contest; it was all those things, but more importantly it offered the opportunity for spectators to experience a passionate attachment to the thing-as-identity. As the game unfolded, each pass, tackle, foul, refereeing decision, shot and goal became an occasion when identity and identification was brought to life, intensified and experienced. This was manifested as joy if the team won, and despair if they lost; pride if they struggled heroically against overwhelming odds, but rage if they were cheated by (what was perceived as) incompetent or corrupt officiating; fear if that defeat took them into the relegation zone, and hope and anticipation if they moved on to the next round of the FA Cup and a fixture against a hated rival. Second, this identification with the team (and sometimes the players) as embodiments of the community was enhanced when the team did well, and brought the community into public and media prominence (by making a cup final, doing well in the league, having a player picked to represent the national team). In this way the success of the team testified to and demonstrated the value of the town or city.

Another important discursive change that came with this mix of professionalism and commercialism was that the status of players became problematical, and the focus of intense debate and discussion. Within public school athletics and amateur Victorian sport a player's status was relatively straightforward: he was part of the team, and his motivation and commitment were unquestioned. In early professional football it was presumed or required that players came from the area, or had some strong local affiliation or history; or if they were imported from elsewhere there was an expectation that they would perform as if there was an affiliation (for instance, by way of playing for that club throughout their career). As professionalism entrenched itself, and players were increasingly treated as commodities, the question of the status of professional football as simultaneously a form of community identity and a business became more pronounced.

Central to this problematic was the issue authenticity: a football team merited its status as a privileged cultural form because it constituted an authentic extension of the community. However, if this relation between team and place, and by extension between team and supporters or fans, was to be considered and experienced as genuine, then there needed to be an appropriate performance of commitment both ways. Supporters were expected to stick with the team through thick and thin (turning up for games even when the team was losing), but concomitantly the team and the players were expected to perform as if that attachment was reciprocated. Paradoxically enough in contemporary football, where the relation between players and teams is largely a commercial arrangement, there is even greater emphasis placed on the performance of an authentic commitment. So on their debut, new players will kiss the emblem on the team shirt in a particularly demonstrable and public manner; it is an empty performance, but a necessary one that cites what for football was a foundational act of mutual identification.

Sport in transition

We can see, from the example of football, that there were significant differences, as well as continuities, between and across the discursive formations that produced and animated public school and Victorian sport. Public school sport was not colonized by or subject to the field of power because it was in effect a subset of the field of power; in other words, its main function was to reproduce and naturalize the dominant status of cultural elites. The value of public school sport, and its consanguinity and identification with regard to the field of power, meant that its autonomy was safeguarded, not least because there was no place, opportunity or incentive for capitalism or the media to challenge that situation. Victorian sport as a cultural field inherited the same discourses, connections, functions, imperatives and networks as public school sport, which meant that to some extent it also inherited its autonomy. However, two factors did leave it vulnerable to challenge and change.

The first of these was the diversity of the set of activities that were eventually gathered together under the name of sport. While ex-public school students could write the rules, standardize dimensions and conditions, draw up the fixture lists and decide who was eligible to play with regard to most sports, each of those had a history which was either distinct from or largely incommensurate with regard to athleticism. Football had always been violent, chaotic and attracted participants from a wide demographic. Boxing was even more violent, dependant on spectators and notorious for its gambling culture. Horseracing tolerated the lower classes, who were an important part of what was in fact an industry as much as a sport, regardless of royal and aristocratic patronage, and it was subsidized by gambling. Rowing and athletics had been popular among the lower classes, and had a history of professionalism. Cricket, even though kept in line by the MCC, had long been characterized by gambling, professionalism and a reliance on spectatorship. What this meant was that the discursive hegemony of athleticism was anything but natural, no matter how widely, frequently and intensely it was naturalized; it remained as something of a foreign discursive imposition that sat uneasily alongside popular sporting discourses, cultures, subjectivities and practices.

The second factor, already referred to in our discussion of football, was the widening appeal of sport, which in turn attracted the interest, and facilitated the involvement, of both the media and capitalism. In some sports this popularity was predominantly to be found within the middle class (golf, cricket, athletics, cycling); but in the case of football it involved the widest possible class demographic. This development was characterized by a number of features: at a basic level it involved professionalism, gate takings and spectatorship, but it also led to an increase in the demand for and the diversification of commodities in the form of sporting and leisure goods (tennis racquets, fishing lines, running shoes, balls, clothing). Equally importantly, by the end of the nineteenth century the popularity of sport had drawn the attention of the newspapers, who were increasingly willing to devote space to sports stories (facilitating discussion and debate about sporting issues and events), and to insert themselves into the field by informing readers about and helping to develop an interest in, identification with, and literacy with regard to, sports, teams, players, traditions and forms of spectatorship. The role of the media in sport had a modest beginning (newspapers started to sponsor events, for example), was both distrusted and resisted by controlling bodies up until the 1980s, and as was the case with the commoditizing of sport it caught on and was accepted more quickly in the United States than in Britain and the Commonwealth. However, by the end of the Victorian period there was in place an incipient sport–media nexus.

Conclusion

By the late nineteenth-century sport was established in Britain as a separate and relatively autonomous cultural field: It had the bureaucratic apparatuses, discourses and self-narratives to articulate itself (what it was and meant, what its values and social functions were, what was inside and outside the field), both to its various constituencies and institutions, and to the field of power. Once established it become the site of ongoing struggles over its identity: internally, as evidenced by the amateur–professionalism debate; and externally, to the extent that it had to negotiate, and was strongly inflected by, its close relationships with powerful fields such as business, politics and the media.

This developing set of relationships between sport and other influential fields brought about two main changes. First it effected a transformation of the forms of cultural work that sport was asked to perform or took on. Second and by extension it also inflected and increased the set of discourses that constituted the discursive regime of sport. This process was accentuated once sport moved beyond its original cultural, social, gender and geographical borders: football and other sports had not just colonized Victorian England; they had also been exported throughout much of the British Empire and to the Americas, had stimulated a European-led revival of the Greek Olympic games; and were being taken up, tentatively, in Africa and Asia. At the same time in Britain a middle-class female demographic was attempting to negotiate and challenge the discourses of masculinity that had been naturalized within and defined the field of sport since its inception. By the beginning of the twentieth-century sport was well on its way to establishing itself as a dominant global cultural form, and it had been taken up by groups and communities far removed from the elites of English public schools and universities.

CHAPTER FIVE

Gender and sport

Introduction

The sporting revolution of the nineteenth century was, to all intents and purposes, 'a male phenomenon' (Guttmann 1978: 78); and this state of affairs has continued, to a marked extent, through to the twenty-first century. This does not mean, however, that the socio-cultural work and functions of sport, and the effects that they produced, did not extend to women: both terms in the male–female binary are dependant upon and inflected by their relation to the other term, and so any work that is done with regard to the categories of male and masculinity also informs and changes the meanings of the concepts of female and femininity. The relation between the field and discourses of sport and the meanings and values associated with gender categories was neither the same for, nor was it necessarily continuous and consistent with regard to, each category. Sporting discourses, however, were and remain highly influential in determining how men and women were understood and valued, the functions and roles that were allocated to them, and the different forms and performances that were associated with normative accounts and templates of gender.

Any genealogy of the relation between sport and gender needs to start with a consideration of athleticism and English public school system, and its role in the construction of 'a new kind of masculinity in which the distinguishing characteristics of the male sex were not intellectual or genital but physical and moral' (Holt 1989: 89–90). Victorian school sport, and by extension sport throughout the Victorian period and beyond, clearly functioned both as a set of sites which privileges men and disqualifies the value of women, but which also normalized, authorized and universalized particular versions and performances of masculinity. So in elite girls' school, would-be ladies either exercised rather than participated in sport, or they played sports that were strongly gendered, being considered as occasions of social interaction (lawn tennis), non-fatiguing (croquet) or divorced from the ethos of team competition (golf, riding) (Hargreaves 1987; Tranter 1998). Women who attempted to dispute this arrangement effectively disqualified themselves as women – certainly as ladies; Hargreaves has pointed to the hardly coincidental overlapping of sport as an emerging bastion of masculinity, and the rise of the suffragette movement (1987: 79).

Public school sport and masculinity

The question of the relation between Victorian public school discourses of sport and masculinity is nuanced and complex. On the one hand there is a strong emphasis on some sports that demanded not just teamwork, but were openly brutal and violent, such as the various versions of football. Masculinity was therefore to some extent discursively manifested in the strong, hard and muscular body; the body that could both endure and give out violence and pain. On the other hand no one was more suspected, watched, despised and derided than the boy who failed to display an interest in or willingness to subject himself to the rigours of sport. To give evidence of intellectual pursuits and airs achieved the opposite work of engaging in and committing to sport; it threatened the removal of recognition, and by extension of the status of subject. At the same time Guttmann (1996) has pointed to the apparent contradiction whereby public school sport both produced an anti-effete, hegemonic masculinism, while simultaneously being one of the few cultural sites where the male body was the legitimate object of the male gaze. That this gaze was at least implicitly erotic, or suspected of being so, can be seen in the suspicion that was directed towards the more aesthetically disposed enthusiasts of public school sport such as Pater, described by Jenkyns as 'loitering wistfully at the edge of the playing fields' (1980: 225).

This sports-driven, public school masculinism was inflected by three additional and apparently antithetical orders of discourse, which:

> became enmeshed . . . imperial Darwinism – the God-granted right of the white man to rule, civilise and baptise the inferior coloured races; institutional Darwinism – the cultivation of physical and psychological stamina at school in preparation for the rigours of imperial duty; the gentleman's education – the nurturing of leadership qualities for military conquest abroad and political dominance at home. In this amalgam Christianity came out second best. The triad resulted in 'Darwinism misinterpreted as the survival of the most belligerent rather than the most adaptable'. Bertrand Russell believed . . . that he could discern the precise relationship between imperialism, Darwinish and the English

gentleman. In the public schools, he declared, physical fitness, stoicism and a sense of mission were carefully nurtured, kindliness sacrificed for toughness, imagination for firmness, intellect for certainty; and sympathy was rejected because it might interfere with the governing of inferior races. (Mangan 1981: 136)

Mangan has drawn attention to the manner in which these 'apparently irreconcilable systems of belief' functioned as 'uncomfortable but actual ideological bedfellows' (135) embodied in Victorian masculinity. The violence, aggression and ruthlessness of both public school sport and colonial wars was always redeemed and in a sense depoliticized by the performance of the right form, involving 'victory within the rules, courtesy in triumph, compassion for the defeated' (135). Richard Holt has suggested that because masculinity continued to occupy a hegemonic position in nineteenth-century British society, these variations within Victorian discourses of manliness have been overlooked by gender theorists:

A greater degree of self-control was expected from Victorian men than from their forebears . . . in general the control of temper, desire, and affection was recommended. At precisely the moment when the new norms of maleness were coming into force, the incarnation of the opposite of 'manliness' was defined in the form of homosexuality, which for the first time was . . . designated a crime in 1885. The homosexual . . . was thought to have various . . . distinctive features . . . 'pale, languid, scented, effeminate, oblique in expression' . . . all that a sportsman was not. The legal battle between the Marquess of Queensberry, the man who had given his name to the modern rules of boxing, and Oscar Wilde . . . over the issue of Wilde's homosexual relationship with the peer's son . . . offers an instructive sidelight on the tension between 'natural' and 'unnatural' physicality. The enormous publicity surrounding the trial . . . juxtaposed aestheticism with true manliness and sportsmanship. (1989: 90)

This version of manliness combined physicality, courage, endurance and authorized forms of violence (hacking and charging in football; rucking in rugby), and was overlaid by an upper-class attitude and bodily hexis that communicated control and an unqualified adherence to the ethos of sportsmanship; in other words manliness was less about winning and more about the reproduction of and a commitment to the right form. This discursive regime was replicated and manifested across the field of sport in the second half of the nineteenth century, dominated as it was by rules, regulations and conventions derived from and commensurate with public school athletics. Football in its amateur guise, for instance, was initially both extremely violent and none too serious. Teams that dominated the early years of the FA Cup, such as Old Etonians and Oxford University, and the quintessential amateur side Corinthians, could kick, barge and charge as well as any semi-professional team from the north, but they did so without seeming to be trying too hard, or for a purpose. This manifested itself in a variety of ways. Amateur teams never committed too many players to defence, even when desperately defending a lead. They tended to rely on individual skill rather than a team system, and training was eschewed, as was anything that seemed to vitiate the amateur air of disinterestedness. The famous multi-sportsman C. B. Fry, for instance, declined to score from a penalty because it meant taking advantage of another's mistake. Professional football teams such as Blackburn Rovers and Preston North End, on the other hand, played to a designated set of tactics, were more inclined to use roughness as a means of gaining an advantage, and gamesmanship. The upper-class male always retained a certain distance from the thing, which militated against both a 'win at all costs' attitude and the strong emotional attachments, forms of identification and ways of seeing and experiencing sport associated with partisan spectatorship. As Neil Tranter has suggested, Victorian sport increasingly had to accommodate two versions of manliness which 'remained fundamentally opposed' (1998: 49). In upper- and middle-class sport manliness meant:

> amateurism, self-restraint, strict obedience to rules and active participation rather than passive spectating . . . to the working classes it meant professionalism, a greater emphasis on physical aggression, commitment to spectatorism as much as to playing and a willingness wherever possible to subvert the rules in the interests of winning. (49)

Sport, masculinity and communal identity

The north–south split in English sport that characterized and inflected the transformation of association football in the 1880s, and brought about the split between rugby union and rugby league near the turn of the century, was marked by an ongoing discursive struggle as to what constituted authentic masculinity. Writing of the formation of the rugby league in 1895, Karl Spracklen writes that the split between the codes was at the same time:

> the invention of a culture defined by what it is not: no southerners, no toffs. The Other becomes a stereotype which is identified and excluded . . . It is also . . . about working lads . . . about men. And by identifying a continuous line from the working class of the split to the working class of today's community of 'the game', one hundred years of migration patterns to the north of England are glossed over . . . rugby league, as a historical myth used to ground a northern identity, limits that identity to people who can own and identify with the myth. Hence, the glorification

of the men involved in the split as role models for the men of 'the game' denies access to 'the game' for the large Asian and black populations that live in the areas of the north where rugby league is established. (2001: 72)

The relationship between these two discursive formations varied across time and place. In English sport upper-class manliness retained its hegemonic status, and helped to naturalize class-based symbolic violence, until the logics and imperatives of sport as media spectacle and business rendered it completely anachronistic; this situation also continued, at an international and institutional level, in those areas of the field of sport dominated by the ethos of English athletics (cricket, rugby, athletics, tennis, rowing). In certain colonial contexts it served the purpose of justifying, explaining and mirroring political, social and cultural inequalities and injustices. In the West Indies and India, for instance, the denial of political rights to the colonized went hand in hand with their exclusion from positions of power, as players or administrators, in the sport of cricket. In the case of the West Indians the situation could be explained in terms of an inappropriate or non-authorized overperformance of manliness that supposedly militated against rational self-control and responsibility; with Indians it was a question of the denial of their capacity for 'virile nationalism' (Appadurai 1997: 91) demonstrated and asserted at the level of bodily competition. In both cases the exemplar of all value was the Englishman, or at least the Englishman raised, moulded and perfected by the culture of athletics, sportsmanship and cricket. As C. L. James writes of his upbringing in the West Indies, this exemplar was simultaneously a 'limitation on spirit, vision and self-respect' and 'the source of all light and leading, and our business was to admire, wonder, imitate, learn; our criterion of success was to have succeeded in approaching that distant ideal – to attain it was, of course, impossible' (1963: 38–9).

In Australian cricket, on the other hand, the status of the codes of masculinity were largely reversed: the assertion of a more pragmatic and aggressive masculinity (not just in terms of batting and bowling, but also at the level of captaincy and spectatorship) could be read as a retort to 'the sanctimonious and patronizing way in which they were regarded by the English' (Appadurai 1997: 91). However, in all cases sport authorized, naturalized and reproduced certain discourses and performatives of masculinity that facilitated the workings of colonial power by organizing and designating who was manly and thus, by extension, a full human subject. As Patrick McDevitt writes 'Games played as defined by English rules and standards set the British and their subjects apart from effeminate continental Europeans, subjugated Africans, and effete Asians' (2004: 2).

An interesting counter-example of the relation between colonial sport and discourses of masculinity can be found in the situation in Ireland from the late nineteenth century through to the period after the civil war, which to a certain extent extended up to the end of the twentieth century. Irish nationalists deliberately rejected English sport and its discourses of masculinity because they were seen, not unreasonably, as an extension of the colonialist apparatus that denigrated Irish culture and identity, and privileged British cultural forms as more civilized, valuable and virile. The Gaelic Athletic Association and its games, and the meanings and significances that were written into them, were counternarratives to British athletics; they took on the function of revitalizing Irish pride, self-respect and assertiveness, and of producing masculine bodies that were differentiated from the bodily hexis associated with the recent history of poverty and famine. The GAA games:

> produced an image of Irish masculinity of which the nationalist community could be proud . . . To a greater degree than in many other games, the everyday coverage of Gaelic sports was couched in gendered language and the issues surrounding Irish 'manhood' implicitly and explicitly dominated the commentary. (McDevitt 2004: 16)

There is a considerable history of specific sports standing in for national or communal masculinity. The discursive relationship between white and African-American masculinities in the United States, for instance, has been inextricably linked in with heavyweight boxers such as Jack Johnson, Gene Tunney, Joe Louis, Max Schmeling, Rocky Marciano, Floyd Patterson, Sonny Liston, Muhammad Ali, and most recently Mike Tyson. The aggressive and sometimes quite intimidating play of the West Indian cricket teams of the 1980s and 1990s, embodied in 'hard' figures such as Colin Croft, Viv Richards and Curtley Ambrose, constituted an altogether different template of manliness from what was represented by supposedly 'softer' Englishmen such as the cultivated David Gower and the cerebral and cross-dressing Mike Brearley. The NFL has traditionally, if unofficially, prescribed that the characteristics associated with African-American masculinity – strength, athleticism, physical intimidation – were unsuited to the qualities required for the role of quarterback, which emphasized the analytical skills, intelligence and leadership of a (white) Peyton Manning or Tom Brady. Scotland's long standing football international with England were occasions when, much like Gaelic games, national masculinity could be reasserted within a context of post-colonial English hegemony. In Australia the relation between the four main football codes – Australian rules, association football, rugby league and union – has been characterized by media and fan discourses that associate the other code(s) with versions of a failed or inappropriate masculinity: for instance, association football is designated as an effete sport, played not by real men but by migrants and homosexuals; rugby league players, on the other hand, are represented as clinging to an unreconstructed, anachronistic and primitive working-class masculinity.

Sport and masculine performativity

The issue of what constitutes an inappropriate overperformance of masculinity varies for one context to the other. A case in point is the American heavyweight boxer Mike Tyson. Boxing itself is a sport of both excessive and problematical, as well as mythic, discourses and examples of masculinity. Tyson embodied all of these features: he was unashamedly violent and brutal, and seemed to have no qualms about, and even seemed to enjoy, inflicting pain and physical beatings on his opponents. Within the field of sport, and across the commercial media, Tyson's persona was largely celebrated: the enjoyment of violence, while not socially sanctioned, was justified and contextualized in terms of certain privileging of boxing as keeping alive an authentic and primeval form of manliness – man as warrior – that was being lost through the influence of civilizing discourses and values. Then in 1991 Tyson was convicted of raping 17-year-old Desiree Washington. At his trial, Tyson made little or no attempt to play down his masculinity: he boasted that he found it difficult to keep his hands off attractive women, and tried to have sex with as many of them as possible. Tyson's performance was an example of how an acceptable performance of masculinity could quickly become illegitimate: instead of being linked to the role, tradition and value of the warrior, Tyson's appetite for violence was now represented as an altogether unacceptable, atavistic reversion to a precivilized state.

While the field of sport provides discursive templates with regard to normative masculinities, this does not mean that its own authorized performances of masculinity will always be in keeping with, or acceptable to, the wider socio-cultural field; nor does it mean that what is unacceptable to the socio-cultural field will be excluded from or lack cultural capital within all areas of the field of sport. The process whereby sporting masculinities cross over into, or are inflected by, other cultural fields is a complex one. However, the heroic and near mythic status of sport and sports stars in popular culture means that sporting contests and heroes are easily transformed into socio-cultural typologies: examples include the black football coach who helps bring about racial reconciliation and understanding (*Remember the Titans*); the fallen sports star who is redeemed through working for and rediscovering his affinity with the downtrodden (*The Longest Yard*); and the baseball fan who reanimates the community through the ideals and ethos of sport (*Field of Dreams*). It is easy to understand how the main characters in fictional boxing films such as *Raging Bull* and the *Rocky* series enjoy considerable and relatively non-reflexive popular acceptance and identification: they demand to be read as both ordinary and extraordinary men. They are ordinary in the sense that their backgrounds, tastes, weaknesses and aspirations are of and recognizable by the people. However, they are also extraordinary in the sense that a strong willed disciplining and fashioning of their bodies as highly effective machines for inflicting and enduring violence allows them to achieve success and earn glory and financial rewards, and thus escape and transcend the limitations imposed by class and ethnicity. In the scene in the movie trailer for the first *Rocky* film, Sylvester Stallone goes on his early morning run through the markets and backstreets of a heavily industrialized, working-class Philadelphia; as he runs through these locations he simultaneously differentiates himself from the people (his body is strong, powerful, fit, athletic and muscular) and connects with them (a vendor throws him an apple, he is recognized and cheered on by workers). Stallone's run, which in itself exemplifies the process of the disciplining and overcoming of the body, culminates in the famous ascent of the steps up to the Philadelphia Museum of Art, where he dances around with his arms raised in triumph while the music builds to an emotional crescendo. This typology was disseminated and taken up, presumably mainly by working-class men, who identified with and embraced the notion of the male, working-class body as teleology. I remember playing a game of competition squash, in the early 1980s, against an opponent whose bodily hexis was clearly modelled on the character of Rocky, and who repeated lines from the film, and directed them both at himself and myself, throughout the game.

A 'hard' and unreconstructed masculinist culture is generally more prevalent in traditional body contact sports such as boxing, American football, rugby league and union, Australian rules and ice hockey. In these sports, sportsmanship and the ethos of athleticism is very much a secondary or tertiary discourse: authentic masculinity is generally articulated in terms of the ability or willingness to inflict and endure physical violence. In these sports there is very little discursive room to move, and any action, sensibility or manifestation of bodily hexis that strays too far from this path is suspect. A good example of this discursive culture in action can be found in the American film *Slapshot*: the film has taken on an iconic status, especially and predictably in Canada, because of the comic, ludicrous, extravagant and largely gratuitous acts of violence (punching, high sticking, charging, elbowing) committed by the comic protagonists the Hanson brothers. In the film the team's fortunes improve as it embraces the Hanson's way of playing, both in terms of results and crowds. Their season culminates in a finals game against opponents who match their violence, but in the middle of various brawls, fights and acts of bloodshed the team's lone talented player, sick of their violent style of play, arranges for the arena organist to play the tune to 'The Stripper', while he skates around the rink and removes his clothing in time to the music, one piece at a time. The female fans in the crowd respond with enthusiasm, but some of the hockey players are openly disgusted. The message, as far as ice hockey is concerned, is straightforward enough: real men partake in, inflict, endure and enjoy violence, but anything that brings an element of sexuality or eroticism onto the rink, or which produces virile masculine bodies as objects of sexual desire, is simply sickeningly perverse.

At the other end of male typologies, and more recently, we can point to the post somewhat androgynous and certainly metrosexual bodies of sportsmen such as David Beckham, Christian Ronaldo and Rafael Nadal, all popular cultural male icons. What is interesting about their cases, however, as distinct from earlier iconic male sports stars such as George Best and Muhammad Ali, is that their identities and representations, particularly in advertisements, are both highly sexualized and eroticized: Best was fashionable and Ali was controversial, but Beckham, Ronaldo and Nadal are first and foremost erotic objects. They are also exemplifications of the notion, prevalent in late capitalist commodity culture, that the body is simultaneously the limit, essence and culmination of identity-as-value. As Baudrillard writes:

> In the consumer package, there is one object finer, more precious and more dazzling than any other . . . That object is the body . . . The body is a cultural fact . . . the mode of organization of the relation to the body reflects the mode of organization of the relation to things and of social relations. In a capitalist society, the general status of private property applies also to the body, to the way we operate socially with it and the mental representations we have of it . . . the current structures of production/consumption induce in the subject a dual practice, kinked to a split . . . of his/her own body: the representation of the body as capital and as fetish (or consumer object). (2003: 129)

The sexualizing and eroticizing of the female sporting body has a long and sustained history, from Suzanne Leglen to Anna Kournikova; but this has not been the case with men. What the various audio-visual advertisements, featuring a scantily clad Christian Ronaldo or Rafael Nadal parading, almost pornographically, for a desiring gaze (presumably both hetero- and homosexual), demonstrate is the incorporation of the male body, and in particular the male sporting body, into an order, first, of desire and consumption; and second, the transformation of the taut, defined, athletic and aestheticized (but not overtly muscular) male body as erotic and cultural capital.

Four main points follow from these examples, and they are points that can be extrapolated across the history of the relationship between the field of sport and discourses of masculinity. First, because sport is an idealized and (socially) magical field of activity that simultaneously distances itself from, while also representing, the everyday world and its communities, it is well placed to embody and play out, at a mythical and heroic level, the tensions, conflicts and dramas of the socio-political field. Second, because sport is one of the few cultural forms that puts the body on public display as proof of moral and ethical strength, virtue, control, authenticity and achievement, the sporting body takes on the status of unambiguous and relatively transportable value. Third, sport is closely associated with, and one of the main socio-cultural sites for, the production and naturalization of masculinity-as-value. Fourth, and following closely from the previous points, certain sports become particularly important and privileged sites for identifying, exemplifying and performing what constitutes, at a given time and place, a normative (bodily) discourse of masculinity. The male sporting body, whether it is found in and a product of Gaelic, American, Australian Rules or association football, boxing, rugby league or union, cycling or ice hockey, exerts a considerable influence over how maleness is understood, represented and performed across the wider socio-cultural field.

Sport and discourses of femininity

As Bourdieu has pointed out, sport was largely 'conceived as a training in courage and manliness' (1991: 360); however, it involved a training in, and a naturalizing of, a very specific notion of masculinity, one that privileged violence as control, aggression, endurance, and the ability to tolerate pain over interests in, and literacies and dispositions with regard to, high learning, art and intellectualism. Women, on the other hand, were originally excluded from, or limited in their membership of, the field of sport. Consequently sporting discourses both informed, in their absentia, discourses of the feminine (the feminine was that which was not, or the opposite of, sport-as-masculinity) and removed sporting women into altogether other categories (as honorary men, but also as non-normative, devalued and inauthentic women).

Women's involvement in organized sport in England in the nineteenth century was clearly limited by a strongly held perception, often supported by scientific and medical discourses and authorities, that their participation in most forms of physical exercise was harmful to their health and child-bearing capacity, not to mention degrading to their femininity. There was also a strong moral discourse that militated against female participation in sport: woman who cycled were often presumed to be and regarded as promiscuous, partly because to be dressed comfortably for any sporting activity was to be dressed in a less than decorous manner, or to be dressed 'like a man'. To a significant extent the bodily hexis of sport was discursively produced and naturalized as being antithetical to femaleness; as Jennifer Hargreaves points out, for some time many women could or would not take proper part in equestrian or bicycling activities because 'To ride astride (or have the legs apart) was considered to be provocative and to symbolize sexual abandonment' (1994: 89). Where women were allowed into sports without causing a scandal, they were limited to a small number of approved and mainly recreational activities, and even here their participation was predicated on them taking up roles and activities, and wearing clothing, that clearly signalled that their status and functions were anomalous, passive, perfunctory, social and decorative:

> Women's recreation embodied the characteristics of passivity and subordination . . . They played 'gentle', respectable games, exemplified by croquet and its indoor derivations . . . Women from the middle and upper classes would be seen in flamboyant wasp-waisted dresses, displaying themselves as ornamental, inactive players . . . Brian Dobb's book . . . Edwardians at play contains fifty illustrations, but there is only one depicting a female participant . . . She is undoubtedly wearing a corset . . . and even with a racket in her hand looks unable to move more than an inch or two in any direction. (53)

The sports that did allow for or did not strongly problematize female membership or participation tended to be upper- and middle-class sports such as tennis, hockey, croquet, badminton, golf and various equestrian events (show jumping, hunting). As with men, women's sport was organized and played in, and formalized and bureaucratized through, elite educational institutions and their members and graduates, although progress was considerably slower than with male organizations. In the last decade of the nineteenth century, women took part in English and Irish university sport (101), and 'games for females which were taken up in schools, colleges and clubs included lacrosse, rounders . . . netball and . . . in the closing years of the century, cricket. However the official governing bodies of these women's games were formed much later . . . lacrosse in 1912; rounders in 1923; netball . . . [and] cricket in 1926' (102).

Both Baron de Coubertin and the IOC (and its all-male members) were generally opposed to the participation of women in sport: as well as the usual moral and health-related objections, Coubertin 'disapproved of women's involvement in public competitions' because the male spectators 'who gathered for such competitions didn't show up to look at sports' (Guttmann 1991: 163). Coubertin's rarely referred to women's sport, but when he did he tended to reproduce a sexist derived from British athletics (and largely accepted by the IOC membership). This sexism was most obviously manifested, at a discursive level, in his disqualification of the female body as suitable for athletic competition, and the linkage he drew between women's participation in the games and the evils of spectatorship and populism:

> His criticisms were essentially based on the biological differences between the sexes and comprised two main arguments. First, and most important, he argued that women were not physically made for athletic activity . . . Women, to his mind, were like other 'weak' members of

society – children, the elderly, and the sick – and were best suited for physical education . . . Moreover, Coubertin believed that women's athletic 'exhibitions' were a distinct threat to the spectators' morals. Noting that athletic clothing was lighter than ordinary dress, he was concerned that the sight of women's nearly nude bodies would arouse . . . primordial passions . . . A clear danger was thus that the spectacle of the lightly clothed female body would become more attractive than the athletic performance itself. (Carpentier and Lefevre 2008: 26)

James Sullivan, the American organizer of the St Louis Olympics, ensured that 'archery was the only sport in which women were allowed to compete' (Guttmann 1991: 163). A significant battle did erupt regarding the inclusion of women's athletics in the 1932 games, after a *New York Times* article complained about the unfortunate sight of exhausted and breathless women at the completion of the 800 metre race in Amsterdam in 1928 (Guttmann 1991). Notwithstanding their concern, shared by various American sporting and physical education organizations, women were eventually allowed to run, jump and throw, as well as swim, skate and fence at the Los Angeles Olympics in 1932; however, the 800 metres for women was not reintroduced into the Olympic games until Rome in 1960. Well into the twentieth century:

women's sporting roles were heavily constrained by norms that had been established during the nineteenth-century debates over medicine and anatomy. These had limited women in a number of ways. First, women were pushed into certain sports deemed appropriately feminine, essentially those emphasising aesthetics and grace over strength and speed. Second, team games developed in a limited way in parallel to rugby and football at boy's schools, but these typically involved less direct physical contact between players than the male team games . . . and . . . attempts to establish women's football and rugby teams were resisted by male authorities in those sports . . . Third, some sports were deemed appropriate for both sexes, but were generally diluted to accommodate women's perceived weaknesses: lawn tennis, with its three-set matches for women and five for men . . . women's hockey, with matches lasting for sixty minutes, men's for seventy; and athletics . . . keeping female athletes out of longer distances and the heaviest throwing events. (Polley 1998: 92)

These developments were not inevitable nor without countermovements and histories. Women's cricket was quite active during the Georgian period (Sandiford 1994: 44), and despite going into decline in the 1830s it started to regain popularity in the 1880s, predominantly in and through the universities; however, although female students were able to play approved sports such as tennis, croquet, badminton and hockey without too much opposition, they were discouraged 'from playing at the manly sport of cricket' (Sandiford 1994: 44). The story was similar with regard to football: the promise of incipient women's football competitions being played in England and Scotland (Goldblatt 2007: 180) was negated, at the end of the century, by a strong (male) institutional backlash fuelled by 'social, medical and sporting commentators' claiming that that physical sports such as football 'was detrimental to women's health' (180).

Women's sport

There were three main factors which to some extent helped to denaturalize the exclusion, trivialization and denigration of, and the opposition to, women's sport. The first was the gradual taking up of sport, as both participants and spectators, by a wider demographic of women. While the growth in women's cricket was limited to elite-educated upper-class women, other sports such as athletics, swimming, hockey, squash, badminton and golf appealed to, and gained participants from, the burgeoning suburban middle class. With regard to golf, for instance, Richard Holt points out that in the post-Edwardian period:

> Women were admitted . . . in significant numbers . . . There was no shortage of middle-class women with time to spare . . . During weekdays ladies might outnumber the men at the club . . . Suburban woman . . . was a lady of leisure who might reasonably aspire to break a 100. Golf offered a kind of half-shared, half-segregated suburban activity rather like the bourgeois family in which a strict division of labour existed . . . More importantly, golf fostered a new kind of community life in the suburbs . . . the golfer could forget the troublesome outside world and settle down to enjoy . . . her modest affluence. (1989: 132–3)

Second, the integration of women's events into major international sporting competitions, such as the Olympic and Empire (later Commonwealth) games, meant that women became involved in the (until the 1930s almost exclusively male) cultural process whereby sport functioned as an important site for the playing out of national identities, rivalries, aspirations and triumphs. During the first 60 years of the twentieth century, for example, Australian women were generally far more successful in the Olympic games than their male counterparts; and gold medallists such as Fanny Durack and Dawn Fraser (swimming), and Shirley Strickland, Marjorie Jackson and Betty Cuthbert (athletics), achieved an iconic status normally reserved for test cricketers. In polls of the greatest Australian sports stars, women such as Fraser (who won an unparalleled three consecutive 100 metre freestyle titles), Cuthbert (who won three gold medals at the 1956

Melbourne Olympics), the squash player Heather McKay (the winner of 16 consecutive British Open titles) and grand-slam winning tennis players Margaret Court usually rank in the top ten, along with Donald Bradman and Rod Laver.

Third, and largely as a consequence of the previous point, media coverage of women's sporting events has increased markedly since the 1970s. Once a sports team or competition becomes associated with national or communal prestige, it often attracts greater media attention; this is particularly pronounced if the relevant nation is also an important media demographic. The best example is the case of women's football. The first women's World Cup was played as recently as 1991 and was won by the United States, which has never finished outside the top three teams. Consequently coverage of the women's team in the US media has been on a par with or greater than any American national sporting team, including the much less successful men's football team; this level of coverage has meant that the status of the women's World Cup, along with the Olympic Women's football tournament, has increased not just in the United States, but also in nations with a record of success such as Japan, China, Brazil, France, Sweden, Germany and Canada.

Conclusion

This increased participation of women in sport in the twentieth century has not, however, resulted in a significant change to the discourses of sport, and the naturalized association of sporting activities and athleticism with men. There are two main reasons for this. In the first place, the field of sport was set up by men for men, and the gendered discourses that articulated the field and its values were authorized and reproduced by institutions, rules and conventions that saw the admission of women as a threat and a challenge to what was a privileged space for the production of masculinity: as Richard Holt writes 'How could men be men if women adopted the very activities through which masculinity was defined' (1989: 117). Second, and notwithstanding the case of women's football, the gradual but inexorable incorporation of sport into the field of the commercial media meant that an already strongly masculine set of narratives, values and discourses was being reproduced and refracted within a field which itself had a strong masculine bias, and which saw itself as selling and disseminating sport to predominantly male audiences. This has been accentuated by the tendency of the media to recruit sporting expertise (commentators, analysts, sporting 'talent') almost exclusively from among men, who in turn presumed, and acted as if, they were speaking to other men. In the second part of the twentieth century the commercial imperative to widen the demographic of all media audiences has meant that women's sport has received wider media coverage, that women are increasingly addressed as part of the sporting audience, and that the reproduction of overtly exclusivist discourses, and examples of blatant sexism, are becoming more problematical. However, the foundational discourses of the field of sport continue to exert an influence over the ways in which gender categories are understood both within the sites and institutions of sport, and across the wider socio-cultural field.

CHAPTER SIX

Global sport

Introduction

Prior to the institutionalization and formalization of sport as a cultural field in the mid-nineteenth century, the ensemble of games, pastimes and forms of play that became sports were in no sense a homogeneous entity unified or connected by any shared discourse, ethos or sense of identity. Moreover, these activities could be found in both the restricted and large-scale areas of the field of cultural production, and in some cases this split ran straight through a single sphere of activity. So in the first instance boxing, horse racing, running, rowing and cricket were strongly informed by commercial considerations, and oriented towards the wider public (in terms of trying to attract paying spectators, allowing some form of professionalism and encouraging betting). Cricket had a foot in both camps: it was played, thrived and took on special cultural significance in elite English public schools, and senior matches and teams were often formed by, and for the benefit of, an aristocratic patron; however, matches were often the subject of substantial wagers between patrons, supporters and players, and attracted large crowds of paying spectators. This commercial and financial dimension was quite productive: one of the factors that promoted the development of cricket in Australia, South Africa and New Zealand (but for various reasons, not in Canada or the United States) was the presence of English touring teams made up of notable amateurs and professionals (Birley 2003). At the same time the sport was run by and for an elite (gentlemen) who were largely disdainful of, and separated themselves off from, professionals players, spectators and the media.

During the late nineteenth and early twentieth centuries British sport was introduced into the Americas, Africa, Asia, the Pacific and Europe (Mangan 1999). However, the establishment of sport as a truly global field was dependent upon progress in international governance, bureaucracy and competitions. British sporting bodies were generally wary or disdainful of the internationalizing of sport: England did not play in the FIFA World Cup until 1950, and as late as the 1950s the English and Scottish FAs initially refused to allow their champion team to participate in the European Cup. However, the success and popularity of international competitions such as the FIFA World Cup and test cricket, and in particular the influence of an Olympic discourse strongly inflected by notions of internationalism, universality and modernity, meant that the parochialism and insularity of British sport and sports governance was increasingly out of step with the rest of the sporting world. This sporting parochialism was no more sustainable, in the long run, than the attempts of English public school-dominated organizations (MCC, FA, AAA, BU) to quarantine sport from the lower classes, women, commercial interests and the media.

Just as the development of modern sport in Britain was tied in with historical movements and events such as 'capitalist development, industrialization, urbanisation, and the scientific-technological revolution', so to the global diffusion of modern sports occurred at the same time as 'the constitution of world markets and colonial empires' (Guttmann 1994: 4). The British Empire was largely governed and administered by ex-English public students and Oxbridge graduates, many of whom proved to be the international equivalents of the evangelists who took sport to the British working class. The establishment of sport in the British colonies of Australia, New Zealand, South Africa, India and in the Caribbean relied on the work of these sports enthusiasts: as members of the ruling elites, as administrators, members of the military hierarchy or as teachers in colonial versions of the still exclusive public school system, they had considerable cultural capital, access to financial and other resources, important socio-political and business connections, and the organizational experience and skills requisite for the task. Moreover, they were expected to take the lead in transplanting its cultural institutions and forms. Both football and rugby were introduced into New Zealand between 1860 and 1870 by 'public school émigrés' (Baker 1982: 133), and this was also largely the case in South Africa, Canada, Kenya, Sierra Leone, Uganda and the Sudan:

> From 1910 to 1948, men recruited for administrative work by the Tropical African Service were selected with an eye to 'character', and character was equated with athletic ability demonstrated by the candidate at a 'public school'. Between 1899 and 1952, Eton, Harrow, Winchester and the other elitist foundations supplied more than 90 percent of all the officers in the Sudan Political Service. The administrative attention paid to sport was extreme. R. D. Furse, a sports fanatic who had studied at Balliol College, Oxford, handed out application forms with a special section for sports. Furse was by no means unusual. 'In the Sudan the provincial governor of Kassala, R. E. H. Baily, who had played cricket

for Harrow and Cambridge, used to circulate a leather-bound book among his staff every morning, in which they were expected to indicate against their names the particular form of exercise they would be taking that afternoon.' The men who had won their 'colours' at Oxford and Cambridge were so prominent in the political service that wits referred to the Sudan as 'the Land of Blacks ruled by Blues'. (Guttmann 1994: 64)

Colonialism and cricket

One prominent example was Lord Harris, who became governor of Bombay in 1890 (and was later President of MCC): he 'believed that cricket was a gift of god' and had to be passed on to Indians in order to 'imbue them with Western modes of thought' (Birley 2003: 164). It is unlikely, however, that Harris envisaged or would have approved of the way in which cricket was taken up by and for Indians, and became associated with Indian nationalism. In *Modernity at Large*, Arjun Appadurai devotes a chapter to this relation between colonialism and cricket in India, and the reasons and logics that might explain how cricket took on such a significant cultural role and status:

> It has something to do with the way sport is managed, patronized and publicized; it has something to do with the class background of Indian players and thus with their capacity to mimic Victorian elite values; it has something to do with the dialectic between team spirit and national sentiment, which is inherent in the sport and is implicitly corrosive of the bonds of empire; it has something to do with the way in which a reservoir of talent is created and nurtured outside the urban elites, so that sport can become internally self-sustaining; it has something to do with the ways in which media and language help to unyoke cricket from its Englishness; and it has something to do with the construction of a postcolonial male spectatorship that can charge cricket with the power of bodily competition and virile nationalism. (1997: 91–2)

The success of cricket in India can be best viewed through this framework of colonial cultural politics. Colonial administrators did not expect that cricket (or any other English sport, pastime or cultural form) would serve the same set of functions as it did in English public schools. Allen Guttmann suggests that while cricket may not have been 'intrinsically more susceptible to hierarchical distinctions of social class than other games', it was 'associated, more than any other sport, with the British ruling class' (1994: 39). However, since cricket was sanctioned by the colonial regime, it was far more likely to be played widely at an organized level (because grounds were available, or because elite schools considered it a valuable part of a boy's education), which in turn helped to produce local exponents who could make a living from the game and go on to serve as a focus for spectator interest.

Once cricket had acquired a significant status within colonial India, it was appropriated as both a public marker of cultural identity and a means of furthering social and political objectives. Nationalists, for instance, embraced it because some of their most prominent members were involved in cricket, because of its popular appeal (cricket virtually introduced the notion of mass spectatorship into India), and because games against British teams fuelled patriotic fervour. Appadurai explains this development by way of a twining together of apparently incommensurate characteristics: sport is attractive because it is a derivative of play, and therefore has no social function; while on the other hand it is a means of facilitating the work of power, as well as socio-cultural mobility and identification (and by extension, identity formation). Both in spite of, and in keeping with, the very exclusive political and ideological functions assigned to it by the ruling class in Victorian Britain, sport:

> like all complex and powerful forms of play . . . both confirmed and created . . . sodalities that transcended class. Thus, it was always open to the most talented (and useful) among the lower and middle classes who stumbled into it. Those among the great unwashed in Victorian England who were capable of subjecting themselves to the social and moral disciplines of the playing field could enter into a limited intimacy with their superiors. The price of admission was complete dedication to the sport and, usually, great talent in the field . . . no amount of shared cricket would make an Englishman confuse an Oxford Blue with a Yorkshire working-class professional cricketer . . . It has also been noted that it was the presence of the lower-class players that allowed the Victorian elite to incorporate the harsh techniques required to win while retaining the idea that sportsmanship involved a patrician detachment from competitiveness. Lower-class professional players thus did the subaltern work of winning so that their class superiors could preserve the illusion of a gentlemanly, non-competitive sport . . . This inherent paradox – an elite sport whose code of fair play dictated an openness to talent . . . is a key to the early history of cricket in India. (Appadurai 1997: 92)

Appadurai characterizes cricket as a 'hard' cultural form, by which he means that it comes 'with a set of links between value, meaning, and embodied practice that are difficult to break and hard to transform . . . I would suggest that cricket is a hard cultural form that changes those who are socialized into it more readily than it itself changes' (90). There is a particularly good representation of this in the Indian film *Lagan*, where an arrogant English officer agrees to play a game of cricket against a team of local cricketing neophytes, with the stakes being the onerous taxes imposed on the local village. As the game is played out, two things become apparent. First, cricket is shown as being an ideal means for teaching and training the hybrid collection of Indians (Sikhs, Untouchables, Brahmins, Hindus, Muslims) to overcome their differences and to work and believe in themselves as a team/community: cricket is the 'between us' that will eventually imagine the Indian nation into existence. Second, the system works and delivers: the game is won by the locals when one of the English umpires no-balls the English fast bowler on what should have been the last delivery of the game, allowing the hero one more strike, which he despatches for the winning runs. The English captain is enraged and attempts to intimidate the umpire into changing his ruling, to no avail; this is cricket, and the umpire's identification and loyalty is to the ethos of the game rather than to Britain, the Empire or his race.

Transplanting sports discourse

The connection between sport and national or communal identity seems to have been particularly pronounced in nascent colonial cultures. Sport was characterized by a definite and prescribed ethos, bodily hexis, chain of command, and set of discourses, dispositions, rules and codes of behaviour. Identities, roles, actions, forms of capital and modes of behaviour were relatively unambiguous, which must have held a considerable attraction for communities removed from the certainties and familiarities of home. The socio-cultural role and status of sport as an alternative space where lower-class groups could compete against their supposed betters on even terms also struck a cord in the more egalitarian cultures of Australia and New Zealand. International sport was always one of the few ways in which nations could assert themselves and their value: the victories of Hindu or the West Indian cricket team over their English opponents, the Australian victory over the MCC in the first 'Ashes' series of 1882, and the triumphant New Zealand All Blacks rugby tour of Britain in 1905, all came to be seen as the manifestation of a kind of communal coming of age. Sporting contests provided colonial societies with a stage and an occasion for performing group and national identity: sport meant popular spectacles, instant heroes and occasions of theatrical drama and passion, something that was quickly appreciated, exploited and promoted by politicians, entrepreneurs and journalists.

In countries outside the Empire, where British influence was less institutionalized and more transient, sport still made considerable gains; however, this was not always accompanied by the maintenance of the original discursive regimes and practices. In Europe organized sport was introduced from the 1870s onward, sometimes through English-style public schools, but more usually through the work of 'visiting or resident Englishmen, who largely made up the early organized teams and at first headed the administrative national associations' (Baker 1982: 134–5).

Rugby was only played in a few areas of France, and cricket failed to gain any kind of permanent foothold outside the Empire. Football however, a 'much simpler and inexpensive' and much less elitist game, took Europe 'by storm during the last two decades of the nineteenth century' (134), and competitive leagues were set up in France, Germany, Italy and the Austro-Hungarian Empire. There were temporary exceptions to the inexorable march of sport: in Germany the *Turning* folk gymnastics movement, founded by Friedrich Jahn, established itself as a nationalistic alternative to sport, which was too 'British' for local tastes; and in Sweden another form of gymnastics, with a strong holistic and quasi-medical character, became the dominant form of physical exercise. Early gymnastics and sports enthusiasts sought to address the same imperatives, such as providing discipline, training the body to endure and surpass itself, and improving the health and strength of citizens. However, while gymnastics movements were not 'immune from the tendency to quantify, to seek records, or to encourage competition' (Guttmann 1978: 88), they disdained the 'anti-spirit of noisy championships' (88), opposed the reinvented Olympics, and 'condemned boxing and running and . . . denounced modern sports as semitic' (88).

In South America, British émigrés, businessmen, employers of railroad construction companies and sailors helped set up sporting associations and leagues in Argentina, Brazil, Uruguay and Chile: football in particular 'was irresistible to the Anglophile elites' (Goldblatt 2007: 130) in the late nineteenth century. Other games such as cricket and rugby tended to rise and fall in a manner commensurate with the rhythms of British economic, educational, political and cultural influence and intervention, although Argentina maintained an interest, and developed considerable expertise, in rugby, hockey and polo. Originally sport in South America was institutionalized by Victorian schoolteachers and businessmen, virtually all of whom were products of British public schools and universities. However, once football became established and was taken up at a mass level, and developed its own local clubs, competitions and local forms of allegiance, its culture and discursive tone veered dramatically away from that of British athletics. In Buenos Aires just prior to the First World War:

> over 300 clubs were playing in numerous unofficial and ad hoc proletarian leagues outside the mainstream AFA organization . . . the newspaper reports of the era indicate that gentlemanly amateurism and the ethos of fair play that British and Argentinian elites had found a useful lubricant were being swiftly abandoned by the new working-class and immigrant football of the barrios. At the bottom of the social scale football served as an instrument of power and revenge. Teams that arrived late at matches would be forced to forfeit the games, however plausible their excuses. The neutrality of referees was often questioned, and the safety of visiting players rarely assured. As for the ever increasing numbers coming just

to watch, one observer wrote . . . 'the behaviour of the Argentinian crowd was not an example of an educated public; they were booing and whistling constantly and a number of the crowd descended to even lower depths.' (136)

The extent to which the transplantation of sports produced discursive inflections, shifts or even transformations at a local or international level varied across sports and geographical locations. Football is a good case: as Goldblatt has pointed out, the way football was watched, experienced and played in Argentina, Uruguay and Brazil was tied in with the kinds of cultural work that it performed in those countries. Socio-cultural, economic and political diversification, tension and inequality (played out at the level of race, class, ethnicity and political affiliations) tended to make football a particularly intense experience, both in terms of settling scores and in gaining some redress with regard to power differentials. Moreover, unstable and populist political conditions meant that football served as both a form of circus for the people, and as a privileged site of the manifestation of nationalism, patriotism and political dissent.

Sport in the United States

As sport spread around the world, the discursive tensions, contradictions and cultures that characterized the field in Britain were revisited and renegotiated in every country, nowhere more dramatically than in the United States. A sport–media–business nexus began to develop there in the late nineteenth century, most particularly in baseball, where from the beginning leagues had operated as businesses. While America initially borrowed from and was influenced by British athletics and its discourses, it gradually developed its own version of modern sport. What initially differentiated America from Britain is that the rise of an American equivalent of British consumer society in the late nineteenth century, while producing an attendant increase in the consumption of luxury goods, broadening cultural practices, and the opening up a market for recreational items and equipment (Struna 1997: 17), did not pave the way for the transition to a bureaucratized and professionalized mass spectator sports culture. In Antebellum America 'sporting events at their most organized might attract a few thousand spectators', while 'The most likely form of "sport"' were 'Folk games and recreations' that 'were part of communal preindustrial life . . . (and which) grew out of face-to-face relationships, and expressed the tensions and cohesiveness of particular localities' (Gorn 1997: 42).

The United States did, by the end of the nineteenth century, have a sports culture that was socially pervasive and recognizably modern; but there were significant variations, as well as similarities, with regard to what happened in sport in Britain and America. America, like Britain, underwent a process of rapid industrialization and urbanization that gave rise to massive increases in crime, hooliganism, alcoholism, gambling, prostitution, ill health, social anomie and excessive sedentary work. Proponents of muscular Christianity and civic reformers promoted sport and physical exercise as both an antidote to these vices, and a means of developing the virtues of 'courage, hardihood, endurance and self-control' (Riess 1997: 186). America lacked a large, affluent and influential private school system bent on promoting the benefits of sport; but there was the ideological influence of Tom Brown's Schooldays, which 'had an enormous impact on American educators, intellectuals, and average people, resulting . . . in a sporting boom at universities like Harvard in the late 1850s' (179).

To some extent elite universities such as Yale and Harvard were the equivalent of the English public schools: they were the sites where games were organized, codified and practised within the wider context of a deliberate sporting ethos. Moreover, American college sport was both elitist and predicated on fulfilling class-based imperatives: the upper-middle class young men who attended college and played American football (a game similar to the variant of folk football played at Rugby and Winchester) were simultaneously constituting themselves as part of an influential social network and acquiring the leadership skills that would be required of their class and/or that network membership. College football was to this group what rugby was to public school Englishmen, being:

> the kind of game appropriate for a nation ripe for a clean, violent, virile, yet gentlemanly sport. Coming after the carnage of the Civil War in an era dominated by the social Darwinian concept of the survival of the fittest, football . . . was, in William James' words, a 'moral equivalent of war' that would teach athletes to be 'contemptuous of softness, surrendering of private interest, and (obedient) to command'. (187)

This class-and-sport network copied its English counterpart in establishing exclusive and supposedly rigorously amateur clubs and governing organizations in athletics, swimming, tennis, baseball, football and rowing. Most of these sports had affiliations with, or directly presided over, what was to become an extremely lucrative system of intercollegiate competitions that developed alongside, and largely corresponded to, the railroad networks that spread across the eastern and central United States after the Civil War. College sport was originally dominated by baseball (the first intercollegiate league was established in 1879) and athletics (1875), but by the 1880s American football games between teams from Yale, Harvard, Princeton and other Ivy League institutions were attracting crowds of forty thousand spectators, and earning athletic associations tens of thousands of dollars in gate money. This surge in spectator numbers and revenue was accompanied by an increase in the competitiveness of sporting competitions; negotiations about and agreement on the standardizations of codes, rules and equipment; a concomitant move towards varying levels of (sometimes unrecognized) professionalism; and the kind of displacement of education by sport that characterized English universities in the late Victorian period.

Well before college football was codified and institutionalized in the 1870s, America's other main sport, baseball, was in the process of transforming itself from a derided version of cricket into an incarnation of American cultural identity. A post-Civil War boom led to the formation of numerous professional leagues; reflecting the strong business ethos of these enterprises, changes to the rules of play tended to develop as a consequence of commercial interests and demands. However, while baseball was quickly integrated into the logics and imperatives of the commercial market, it was also simultaneously removed from and set above that market through its close association with a mythical/pastoral world manifested in the 'sounds of summer, the tap of bat against ball, the cries of the infielders, the wooden plump of the ball into the catcher's mitts' (Guttmann 1994: 51–2). Because of its perceived special place in and relation to American culture, baseball remained inalienable, in a legal sense: in a Federal League case of 1922 'the court decided that baseball was an exhibition and not a business in the sense of the Sherman Antitrust Act of 1890' (Guttmann 1978: 97); and this position was reiterated in rulings in 1957 and again in a 1972, despite the Supreme Court consistently denying the same status to boxing and professional football. This development was the product of a configuration of socio-political, technological and commercial factors. At one level it was part of a wider rejection of and a distancing oneself from Britain and its class structures, of which baseball's close relative cricket was the exemplar. But there were other 'contributing factors, such as greater urban concentration enhancing the prospects for spectator sports, and better rail travel facilitating intercity competition' (Vincent 1994: 93). The Civil War and the subsequent mass movement of populations to urban and industrial centres 'traumatically dislocated millions of Americans' (94), and as with their English counterparts in Birmingham, Manchester and Liverpool they found a sense of communal identity and belonging through their involvement in, attendance at and support of local sporting teams.

Probably the most significant cause of the transformation of baseball from sport into discursive myth, however, was the close relationship that grew up, in late nineteenth century, between baseball, the commercial media, and mass communication technologies and networks:

> The nearly universal availability of the telegraph was made more effective in the 1880s by the adoption of techniques to send several messages simultaneously over the same wire. Pool rooms and saloons all over America installed receiving sets to keep their customers up-to-date regarding nationally important baseball scores . . . The establishment of

mass journalism is explainable by the waiting for words by the literate population and the exploitation of techniques for high-speed typesetting and printing. Much of the news came from wire services and the news that increased circulation most was sports news. (Mandell 1984: 184–5)

Prior to the Civil War, and as was the case in Britain, sports news had appeared intermittently in American newspapers and journals, often as an adjunct to social news; but by the 1890s there were separate sports pages. The popularity of sport, and baseball in particular, was given an enormous boost by increased newspaper coverage that often worked in tandem with highly successful public relations campaigns run by sports entrepreneurs such as Albert Spalding. Partly as a consequence of the horizontal integration he developed across his manufacturing and marketing operations, Spalding was a pivotal figure in popularizing sports participation worldwide: he mass produced, promoted and standardized tennis equipment; helped to initiate the bicycle fad at the turn of the century by developing faster, safer and cheaper machines; and represented American sports at the Paris Universal Exposition of 1905. His focus, however, was on baseball: he started out as a player and later became a manager and team owner, a chronicler and historian of the game, a tour promoter and the official supplier of bats and balls to the professional leagues. He also literally brought about a rewriting of baseball history so as to more firmly establish a discursive correspondence between it and American cultural heritage and identity. The game's pastoral associations and national integrity were inscribed and naturalized by way of the invention of a myth of:

> Abner Doubleday and his Cooperstown cow pasture . . . in order to wipe away the memory of the game's actual invention, in its modern form, by a New York bank clerk named Alexander Cartwright. The myth of Abner Doubleday was cut from whole cloth in 1907, when Spalding appointed a commission, chaired by his friend Abraham Mills, to investigate the origins of baseball. The rigged nationalistic commission which put the undeserving Doubleday in the ludic pantheon was determined to disprove the (correct) theory that baseball was derived from the British children's game of rounders. On the basis of a letter from an octagenarian named Abner Graves, Mills obligingly informed the delighted Spalding that the game was an American invention. (Guttmann 1994: 52)

Conclusion

The situation with turn-of-the-century baseball in a sense epitomized the field of sport as it was developing in the United States, away from and in contradistinction to what was happening in Britain and the British Empire, and to some extent the rest of the world. There were a number of continuities and shared characteristics that continued to mark sport, regardless of where it was located, such as the pervasive and highly influential place of athletics and other forms of exercise within the fields of health and education; the strong identification between communities and local and national sporting teams; the maintenance of a strong discursive commitment to an ethos of fair play and the benefits of agonistics; the development of regular national and international competitions and tournaments; and the internationalizing and/or global networking of governance organizations. However, the early twentieth-century American experience of a strong connection between sport with the fields of business and media was not universally replicated for perhaps another 70 years or so.

At the same time that sport was being transformed into a form of commercial entertainment in the United States, an altogether antithetical movement was developing in Europe, based on the idea of a fusion of classical Greek and English public school athletics. These two movements, one predicated on commercial and media imperatives, the other on a strict adherence to the ethos of competition, fair play, *askesis* and amateurism, were to coexist as the dominant discursive forms of sport in the first half of the twentieth century.

CHAPTER SEVEN

The modern Olympic games

Introduction

In a lecture given at the Sorbonne in November 1892, Baron Pierre de Coubertin announced his plan for reviving the Greek Olympic games, but in modern form. He began the lecture by describing and evaluating the benefits and qualities of the three pre-eminent systems of physical exercise at this time: these were German gymnastics, which involved heavy exercise on fixed apparatuses; Swedish gymnastics, which consisted of mainly light exercises and winter activities; and British sport (Coubertin 2000: 287). He described the benefits that German and Swedish gymnastics had brought to their peoples (the first military strength and preparedness, the second health and well-being), and contrasted this with the situation in France, which he argued had ignored the health and fitness of its population, resulting in military defeat at the hands of the Prussians in 1870. For Coubertin, France needed to find to find a way of producing strong, healthy, disciplined men who could match the 'military athletes' 'born in Berlin' (288). At the same time he suggested that military imperatives only constitute one aspect of the work that needed to be done to reinvigorate 'the blood of France' (288); what was also lacking was a set of cultural forms that provided discipline and improved general health, but also instilled a general moral robustness and esprit de corps within a community degraded by the examples of the 'weaklings and libertines' (288) of town and court.

The influence of English athletics

Despite his appreciation of the value of German and Swedish gymnastics, Coubertin had reservations about both: he felt that the former was quite inflexible and almost exclusively military in its orientation; and that the latter was too focused on health issues and helping 'the sick and the frail', and accordingly lacked an appreciation of or interest in promoting the benefits of play and/and competition. He contended, instead 'that in the whole world, there is not a system more refined . . . towards youth than the current English system' (294) of athletics, which is:

> already taking over the world . . . sixty years have sufficed for this prodigious transformation. The first workers were less worried about going to school than obtaining some healthy pastimes. They were far-sighted, however. A certain philosophical glow surrounded them: reminders of Greece, respect for the stoic traditions and a fairly clear idea of the services that athletics could render the modern world were not slow in drawing attention to them. They were mocked, but ridicule did not discourage them . . . their work was already under the protection of youth. The universities of Oxford and Cambridge had started to associate themselves with it. There they must have found the seeds of magnificent recovery, a very necessary purification . . . The cause was quickly understood and won. Playing fields sprang up all over England. The number of clubs grew . . . not in the aristocratic quarters, but in the poor and popular areas. Every village has one or two . . . Then, when they left their native land, the sons of Albion took the precious recipe with them, and athletics flowed into the two hemispheres in the most varied of climates. (294)

What gave athletics a significant advantage over gymnastics, for Coubertin, was the extent to which it fitted more comfortably with discourses of progress, rationality, reason, modernity, communication, science and technological innovation. While Coubertin subscribed to the virtues of athletics as a panacea for the failings of French national character during the Franco-Prussian war, simultaneously he dismissed this approach as short sighted, limited and even anachronistic. He felt that narrow parochialism was an inadequate response to the serious issues of the time, such as the intensification of international rivalries and conflicts, widespread social inequality and discontent, the commercialization of everyday life, the evils of industrialization, moral decline, the spread of drunkenness and dissipation, and the spectre of socialism. Athletics, on the other, belonged to and promised to facilitate a progressive future because it was:

> democratic and universal. The first of these characteristics will guarantee its future: anything that is not democratic is no longer viable today. As for the second, it opens unexpected prospects to us. There are people whom you call utopians when they talk . . . about the disappearance of war, and you are not altogether wrong; but there are others who believe in the progressive reduction in the chances of war, and I see no utopia in this. It

is clear that the telegraph, railways, the telephone, the passionate research in science, congresses and exhibitions have done more for peace than any treaty or diplomatic convention. Well, I hope that athletics will do more . . . Let us export rowers, runners and fencers; there is the free trade of the future, and on the day it is introduced within the walls of old Europe the cause of peace will have received a new and mighty stay. (297)

Coubertin borrowed not only the ethos of British athletics, but also its elitist methods of organizing and constituting itself. The International Olympic Committee was set up as a '"self-recruiting body" . . . like the organizing body of the Henley Regattas' (322), with a permanent body of suitable people as 'active members' who would elect or enlist the aid of new members and helpers as circumstances dictated (322). This meant that membership of the IOC was usually restricted to white upper-class men: the first non-white and women members, for instance, were not added until the 1970s and 1980s, respectively (Guttmann 1992: 156).

The IOC also followed the lead of English athletics in its attitude towards professionalism, although what constituted amateurism was constantly being reviewed until its effective abolition as a requirement in 1978 (Guttmann 1992). At an address given in Tokyo in 1940, Coubertin went so far as to insist that with the modern Olympics 'there never has been any such thing as amateurism . . . there is not a single word in the Oath . . . that refers to amateurism' (2000: 521). Despite Coubertin's protestations, however, he was an adherent of the amateur ethos of public school sport and had a distaste for and opposition to professionalism: consequently the IOC defined eligible competitors in terms of rules derived from the Amateur Athletic Association, which effectively disqualified any competitor whose expertise was associated with their employment (Guttmann 1992: 12). Coubertin wrote, somewhat obliquely, that the 'solemnity of the Olympiads' demanded that a greater emphasis be placed on 'the purification of the participants' (265). From the earliest games this issue was the subject of considerable controversy, debate and scandal: the American athlete Jim Thorpe was eventually stripped of the medals he won at the London Olympics of 1912 after it was discovered that he had played semi-professional baseball before competing in the Olympics (Guttmann 1992: 34); and from 1912 onward there was considerable bitterness, particularly on the part of the British, with regard to the status of American athletes on college sporting scholarships.

Hellenism

For Coubertin, sport was continuous with regard to the notion of progress associated with the French Revolution, and constituted a 'discourse of salvation . . . intended to transcend the spatial and temporal dimensions of the social fabric' while aspiring to the 'recovery of the lost agora of Attic cities' (Mattelart 2003: 23). The revival of the Olympic games was also a revival 'of a threefold harmony first outlined in Hellenism' which reconciled the community, the individual and morality (Coubertin 2000: 278). The new Olympics would help to 'give us social peace' (275) by reviving, reincarnating and keeping sacred the spirit of the original Olympics and the ethos and function of the Greek gymnasium: 'sport, hygiene, science and art' (275) would mingle together; and different generations, people of political persuasions, and the various classes would become acquainted and learn 'to esteem one another' through the sharing and appreciating of 'muscular joy' (275).

The revived Olympics were not meant to serve as an anachronism; Coubertin (2000) saw that modern sport offered numerous technological benefits, such as a better and a wider range equipment (the bicycle, racquets, balls, skates), and superior facilities and communication infrastructure. Greek athletics, on the other hand, has something that modern society and sport both lacked: 'the philosophical foundation, the loftiness of the goals, the whole patriotic and religious apparatus that surrounded the festivals of youth' (536). Without the Hellenic ethos and spirit, modern sport would:

> decline into commercialism and into the mud, and we know we must protect it from such a fate at all costs. If we fail to maintain its nobility, the hopes based upon it will be dashed. It will play no role at all in schools, and will have no effect on the life of the community. (536)

In a series of addresses just prior to and after the First World War, Coubertin continually rearticulated this idea of Olympic sport as a privileged space that was superior to, and could effect an improvement of, society and culture. The 'virtue of the Greek formulae' had been 'perfected by Anglo-Saxon civilization' (272): British public school athletics had established 'a happy equilibrium between the inequality introduced by nature among men and the equality which legislation seeks to impose' (273). His argument was that whereas social and political injustice was both long term and unjustifiable, the inequalities of sport were 'transient and justified' (273), since they were derived from and produced on a level playing field. Further, the inequalities of sport were a catalyst for harmony and improvement, rather than disaffection and institutionalized abjection:

> Inequality in sport is based on justice, because the individual owes what success he obtains only to his natural qualities multiplied by his will-power; it is moreover a very unstable inequality, because this ephemeral form of success exacts continuous effort if it is to endure even for a little. These are interesting data for Democracy . . . in sporting circles we see an easy blending of authority and freedom, and above all of mutual help

and rivalry. Now Democracy needs to be able to blend these ingredients . . . Sporting authority is inevitably due to merit recognized and accepted . . . Thus the sportsman has before his own eyes a permanently valid lesson in the necessity of command, control and unity, while the very nature of the comradeship around him obliges him to see in his comrades both collaborators and rivals – which from the philosophical angle seems to be the ideal principle of any democratic society. (274–5)

At a discursive level the early Olympic games, as well as the IOC itself and its rules, categories and conventions 'celebrate an . . . idealised version of Ancient Greece' (Goff 2011: 3), and the games themselves were characterized by the invocation of this line of descent. At the same time, discourses and discursive statements were also the product of a reciprocal line of vision; if the contemporary world looked back to Greece and Olympia for inspiration, Coubertin's Hellenism anticipated and committed to a vision and version of modernity understood as a form of technologically driven progress, rationality and reason. Coubertin's plan for the 'modern Olympic city', for instance, married the idea of a discrete organic community and architecture, modelled on the Greek polis, to 'utopian' architectural ideas of the eighteenth and nineteenth centuries that facilitated communication, differentiation and surveillance (Foucault 2001); while at the same time manifesting a very contemporary upper-class phobia with regard to the idea of the crowd and mass society (Mattelart 1994):

[P]rovision would have to be made for a senate building, consisting of a large reception hall and a meeting room for about fifty people, and an administrative building . . . These two buildings would be located within the enclosure, the Altis. In addition, provision would have to be made for the residence of the chief gardener and the residence of the ground keeper, both of whom could act as concierges at the entrance . . . [and] the space needed by the Organizing Committee for the Olympiad . . . sports, art competitions, festivals and presentations, finances and dispute resolutions . . . These premises should be built on the outskirts of the enclosure, in architectural annexes to the city, so that the appearance of the city is not marred, yet the distance between these buildings and the city is not impractical and bothersome. In the same area there should be an expandable sort of hotel . . . Let us note that providing lodging for the public, the spectators, is not at all what we are talking about. The hotel would be built for . . . delegates or participants. (Coubertin 2000: 261)

For the first of the modern games the events were originally divided into five categories: 'athletics and gymnastic sports, sports of combat, equestrian sports, water sports and finally, games as such' (262). Only the first three corresponded to the genre of Olympic events, and that sometimes tangentially or superficially. Most of the sports included had a strong affiliation with British sport: these included track and field events recognized and practised by the AAA, and various forms of fencing, boxing, wrestling, shooting, swimming, rowing, equestrian competitions, polo and the games of football, hockey and tennis. Where there were direct lines of descent from the ancient games (running, wrestling, boxing) the modern standardized and quantified forms prevailed. This dialectic of 'modernized antiquity' was neither consistent nor free from the intrusion of non-sporting logics and imperatives. A marathon race was included in the first of the modern Olympics, based on the distance Pheidippides was meant to have run from the battlefield to Athens, and appropriately enough it was won by a Greek peasant. Excessively violent combat sports such as the *pankration* were excluded, since they were a fatal form of assault waiting to happen. Horse racing was deemed to be too dependent on the ability of the animals; cycling, rather than automobile racing, was considered a suitable replacement. Coubertin (2000) also expressed a desire to introduce activities with no Hellenistic lineage but which had a military application, such as fencing on horseback and the pentathlon.

There were other discontinuities: athletes marched and competed under their national flags; winning times and distances were recorded; a medal (but not points) table was introduced; women were eventually allowed to compete in tennis and golf in 1900, but not in athletics until 1920 (Guttmann 1992: 33); a winter Olympics was introduced at Chamonix in 1920; the familiar Olympic flag (with five rings representing the continents) and the flight of the doves (representing peace) were introduced at Antwerp in 1920; and in keeping with their internationalist orientation, the hosting of the games was rotated rather than left to Greece. In other respects, however, it could be said that the invented traditions, ceremonies and markers of the Olympics were strongly oriented towards antiquity; or at least they constituted a performance of a necessary articulation between the ancient and the modern. Like the ancient Olympics, the modern version incorporated an opening ceremony; athletes were required to recite an oath; the winners received an olive wreath; and a torch relay was eventually introduced at the Berlin games (Keys 2006: 144). Barbara Goff writes that while the modern Olympics 'have not systematically invoked ancient Greece, the medals, posters, and opening ceremonies frequently do' (2011: 8); although with specific regard to the design of the medals, she suggests that there is a history of the 'forcing of the modern into the ancient mould' which 'seems to speak less . . . Greece than to the IOC's consciousness of its own tradition' (9).

Universalism, internationalism and globalization

The Olympic movement's commitment to the legacy of Hellenism and athletics was discursively linked to and commensurate with the wider nineteenth-century innovation of universal expositions and world trade fairs. Mattelart has argued that these institutions performed a number of functions 'Above and beyond the spirit of the imperial times that inspired them' (1994: 43), the most significant of which were the standardization, development and evaluation of different fields and disciplines, and the attempt to institutionalize legal, technical, bureaucratic and communication norms at a global level (44).

This was true with regard to the field of sport: the Olympic games, along with other important global and international sporting events, competitions and congresses, were at the forefront of the global exporting, universalizing, transforming and standardizing of sport in the late nineteenth and early part of the twentieth century. It could be argued that the modern templates, trajectories and cultures of sports such as football, athletics, golf, swimming, cricket and the two versions of rugby were formed at this time, as local rules, affiliations, competitions and traditions came up against and eventually gave way to the twin imperatives of standardization and globalization. This was a gradual and delicate process: in the Athens Olympics of 1896, for instance, the rules and regulations of events varied across sports, with the British AAA, the Societe d'Encouragement de L'Escrime of Paris, the Rowing Club Italiano, the International Cyclist's Association and the All England Lawn Tennis Association presiding over athletics, fencing, rowing, cycling and tennis respectively (Coubertin 2000: 327). Moreover, the liminal and uncertain status of the early games (both Paris in 1900 and St Louis in 1904 were integrated into the infrastructure and events of World Fairs) meant that compromises, anomalies and novelties were a necessary part of the process; the most infamous of these was the inclusion of an 'anthropology day' in 1904, featuring competitions between indigenous peoples of different continents. By 1928, however, most traces of the heterogeneous, the arbitrary and the local had given way to a strong culture of bureaucratization and standardization (Guttmann 1992: 44).

Universalism, internationalism and globalization are discourses that invoke the idea of a progressive modernity, 'the perfectibility of human societies', and the accomplishment of reason via 'the domestication of . . . the irrational, which separates people' (Mattelart 2000: 2). However, as Mattelart points out, they also facilitated and sponsored 'new forms of unequal exchange' (1994: 45) in forms largely indistinguishable from colonialism:

> European criminal anthropology exported its conception of the profile of delinquency and normality to all of Latin America . . . 'Orientalist' anthropologists . . . invited the 'Orientals', in the course of a universal exposition, to see themselves through the mirror offered them by the civilized West. Indian and Pakistani researchers have . . . demonstrated the role played by expositions . . . in the degradation of Indian art and crafts. (45)

In a sense Olympism 'formed part of the colonial project' (Bale and Christensen 2004a: 2), or perhaps more correctly the post-colonial project: the games constituted a regime of physical activity-as-ethos which systematically overturned, replaced and consigned to anthropological study countless cultural activities and forms throughout the world. Henning Eichberg has shown how, as recently as the 2000 games in Sydney, Olympism and post-colonialism continued to function as discursive bedfellows:

> [W]hen the Olympics were arranged in Sydney 2000, the organizers placed a boomerang in the centre of the games' logo. This pre-colonial throwing instrument was presented as symbolizing the idea of a 'multicultural games' and 'cultural diversity in a harmonious society ... united in its patriotism' ... however, one does not find any boomerang throwing in the Olympic sports programme ... in this field of activity, the aboriginal contribution is missing. The absence of 'the other' not only is a question of the instrument ... but also has its roots in the deeper patterns of sportive movement. Boomerang throwing, as well as Aboriginal games ... in general, do not fit ... the pattern of sport. That is why Aborigines may enter into the Anglo-Western sport of Australia, but their own ... culture has no relevance for Olympic ... sport ... From the sportive perspective, the Aboriginal tradition is a non-sport. (2004: 65–6)

Commercialism and nationalism

Mattelart identifies a third aspect of the universalist exhibitions and fairs of the late nineteenth and early twentieth centuries that also quickly became an issue for the Olympic movement, despite Coubertin's efforts to the contrary: the tendency for the events to take on a commercial and popular form, and degenerate into spectacle and entertainment. Mattelart credits sport with making a major contribution to this process, from the launching of the America's Cup yachting challenge at the London exposition of 1850 to the 'cycling and automobile races, marksmanship contests, aeronautic contests, and fencing matches' (1994: 46) that were shared between the exposition and the Olympics of 1900. Coubertin disliked and resisted the attempts made to popularize the games in 1900 and 1904, which he considered a form of vulgarization that detracted from the Olympic spirit and ethos, much as commercialism and excess had ruined the original games (2000: 543). He was not particularly impressed by the large and (over)enthusiastic crowds that attended the first games in Athens. In an address in 1909 he suggested that 'We have grown accustomed to judging the success of a festival by the numbers of those in attendance ... To apply this coarse principle in a permanent and long-lasting way to the Olympic games would be to commit a very serious error' (267). For Coubertin 'the ideal sports spectator is a sportsman on holiday, taking a break in his own exercise routine to follow the exploits of a more skilful or better trained friend' (267).

The continued popular success of the Olympics did not change his position. In an article in 1928 he railed against the culture of spectatorship, and the fact that stadiums were:

> being built unwisely all over the place. Those curious enough to leaf through . . . the Revue Olympic . . . would find warnings against athletics as a show, and the eventual consequences of that approach . . . At the time I said that once seats for forty thousand spectators are built, you have to fill them . . . To draw that crowd, you will need a publicity campaign, and to justify the publicity campaign you will have to draw sensational numbers . . . Almost all the stadiums built in recent years are the result of local and, too often, commercial interests, not Olympic interests at all . . . people are on the attack against the athletes, accusing them of the corruption that has been forced on them for the past twenty years . . . In my view, these oversized showcases are . . . the root of the evil. (184)

The problem of commercialism was tied in with, and to some extent derived from, the function the games took on as sites for showcasing nationalism and international rivalries. The experience of the first games in Athens was celebrated as a new era in Greek history: Coubertin felt that the appreciation of and interest in athletics constituted a 'perfect fever of muscular activity' that would bring 'a notable increase of vigor' among a people who had lost the link with their athletic lineage (359). In 1900 and 1904 the occasions, although marked by partisanship, were insufficiently competitive to excite nationalistic fervour; the Paris games were overshadowed by and lost inside the World's Fair, and the Americans completely dominated events in St Louis, which attracted few overseas athletes. The problem came to a head in 1908, however, when an intense and bitter rivalry developed between British and American athletes, many of the latter of whom were of Irish descent. This resulted in controversies, scandals, accusations of unsporting behaviour and professionalism (mainly directed against the Americans by the British), and open dissatisfaction with the local officials, who were thought to be biased towards their compatriots (Guttmann 1992: 29–30). As Guttmann writes:

> As sports contests, the games of the Fourth Olympiad were quite successful, but they were marred by unusually strident nationalism . . . The most controversial political question of the day was the fate of Ireland (where) . . . the mostly Roman Catholic Irish were still ruled by the mostly Protestant British . . . Irish American athletes were many

. . . As the teams marched into the stadium on opening day, national flags fluttered, but the Stars and Stripes hung at half-mast . . . Many British spectators were convinced that this . . . was a slap in the face for the king and queen . . . When competition began, the officials, all of whom were British, were accused of bias . . . the British press denounced the Americans for their lack of good sportsmanship . . . The *Times* (London) (concluded) that 'the perfect harmony which everyone wished for had been marred by certain regrettable disputes and protests', but the editors took comfort in the illusion that athletes and officials departed London with their friendship unimpaired. (29–30)

International officials were used in Stockholm in 1912, but the issues of nationalism, professionalism and commercialism resurfaced when the games resumed after the war. This period also saw something of a resolution to the question of the status and extent of the participation of women in the Olympics. They were eventually admitted to a limited number of athletic events, and achieved increased participation in other sports, during the Amsterdam Olympics in 1928 (Carpentier and Lefevre 2008: 27). Women were eventually allowed to run, jump and throw, as well as swim, skate and fence at the Los Angeles Olympics in 1932.

The 1932 and 1936 Olympics saw significant changes with regard to how the games were organized, promoted and conducted. In Los Angeles film celebrities were used to help gain and hold media attention, draw crowds, and generally put on a Hollywood-style show; it was probably the first time that the Olympics had been fully incorporated into, and became to some extent dependent upon, a public relations and marketing regime (Guttmann 1992: 50). The 1936 Olympics in Berlin were preceded by an intense and vitriolic debate, and the threat of a boycott, regarding the appropriateness of holding the games in Fascist Germany. The boycott failed, partly because the influential American Olympic official and future IOC President Avery Brundage was convinced that it was 'a conspiracy of Jews or Communists' (60); and partly because the Nazis guaranteed that the selection process for the German team would not discriminate against Jews. Hitler was a late convert to the games and to sport in general. His sympathies and tastes were aligned with German gymnastics: their unabashed nationalism and race-consciousness was closer to his ideals than the discursive universalism of modern sport, which had been condemned by a Nazi spokesperson in 1932 as being 'infested with Frenchmen, Belgians, Pollacks and Jew-Niggers' (54). Unlike gymnastic festivals, however, the Olympic games were prestigious global events that offered an unparalleled opportunity 'to demonstrate German vitality and organisational expertise' (55).

Cashman has written of the Berlin Olympic games that 'Rarely has a sporting event been used so blatantly for propagandist purposes' (2000: 201); Coubertin, on the other hand, thought that it had 'magnificently served the Olympic ideal' (quoted in Guttmann 1992: 70). Placed side by side the two comments support Jean-Marie Brohm's charge that the Olympics had been 'proto-fascist from the beginning, and . . . could be staged to perfection only in a fascist country' (quoted in Kruger 2004: 48). The political tone of the Berlin games simply reprised what was, more or less from the beginning, a salient characteristic of the Olympic movement, and of modern organized sport in general.

This trend has been accentuated since 1960 and 1964 (the Rome and Tokyo games), with the advent of live television and the coverage and the payment of substantial rights to broadcasters. These developments were crucial, for two reasons: first, they sent the Olympic movement, quite irrevocably, down the path of professional, commercialism and the media spectacle; second, the availability of a worldwide live audience upped the ante in terms of Cold War and wider political interest, importance and utility. Moreover, the two developments acted as mutual intensifiers: Rome and Tokyo use the games to manifest their re-emergence as members of the modern international community, and in 1968 Mexico took its own place on the world stage.

The Olympic games as political discourse

Guttmann makes the point that, from here on, athletes behaved as if they were on camera (1992: 105), but the same could be said to their roles as representatives of ideologies and nations. While the expulsion of South Africa from the 1964 games constituted a major and overt political intrusion into the Olympic discourse of autonomy and political disinterestedness, the 1968 games in Mexico City saw the IOC take a stand by expelling Tommie Smith and John Carlos, the gold and bronze medalists from the men's 200 metres athletics race, for their now famous 'raised fist' salute while the American national anthem was playing during the medal presentation ceremony. Smith and Carlos insisted that their action was a protest against oppressive politics, and not just racism in the United States. However, they were ordered out of the Olympic village and eventually expelled from the games at the insistence of IOC president Avery Brundage; when it was pointed out to him that he had made no objections to the use of the Nazi salute during the Berlin games, he justified his position by differentiating between national political gestures (which were allowed) and individual or sectarian ones (which were not) (130). What made this distinction even more notorious was that Brundage and the IOC had made no protest nor taken any action after the Mexican army massacred hundreds of students protesting against the games (129).

After the Second World War, the Olympics became an important site for the playing out of Cold War rivalries: each Olympic games presented an opportunity for the two dominant political and ideological regimes to compete with and outdo each other. This competition took both overt and discrete forms: it focused on results (medals won, world record performances), but it was also played out at the level of the body and bodily hexis. Whether it was in marching, preparing to compete, running, swimming, celebrating, dealing with defeat, being photographed and interviewed, or engaging with the crowd and other athletes, the athlete's body was charged with carrying out, constantly and continuously, the discursive work of the relevant political regime.

The admission of the Soviet Union into the Olympic movement in 1951 had been the catalyst for an overt polticizing of IOC governance, and this also manifested itself in refereeing and judging decisions (most obviously in boxing, gymnastics and diving). In the basketball final of the 1972 Munich games, for instance, a dispute about time keeping which was crucial to the result (the Soviet Union beating the United States) was decided by jurors voting on political lines (138). In the 1970s and 1980s, the playing out of international political disputes effectively replaced Hellenism, athletics and universalism as the raison d'etre of the Olympics. The 1976 games in Montreal were upstaged by African nations protesting again New Zealand's maintenance of rugby contacts with South Africa; the 1984 and 1988 games, in Moscow and Los Angeles respectively, were marred by Cold War-inspired boycotts. In 1968 in Mexico City the police massacred students protesting against cuts to social services to pay for the Olympics; the summer games held in Montreal, Seoul, Barcelona, Sydney, Beijing and London resorted to an 'ethnic cleansing-style' relocation or temporary disappearance of groups (prostitutes, petty thieves, the poor, the homeless) whose presence was considered likely to project the wrong image (Lenskyj 2004).

Ideological and political differences, disputes and competitions were also played out within specific Olympic events, particularly prestigious events that received almost universal television coverage, where the athletic body functioned as a site for comparing, contrasting and evaluating communism and capitalism, socialism and democracy, east and west. By way of example, we can look at the men's 100 metres athletics' finals of 1972 and 1984, won by Valeri Borzov (Soviet Union) and Carl Lewis (United States) respectively. Borzov is very focused at the start of his race, neither interacting with nor acknowledging the crowd or his fellow competitors. As he crosses the line, he raises his arms in victory, then regains himself, and jogs on for another 20 metres without smiling or showing any other sign of celebration; his only action is to motion briefly and unobtrusively to someone in the crowd. Eventually he stops, politely acknowledges his competitors, and lets the media show happen without giving himself to it, or allowing it to intrude on the moment. That moment is Borzov's time and space, but only in the sense that his identity is embodying something that is more than himself; bodily movements, gestures and facial expressions manifest ideals and values altogether commensurate with the discourses of Hellenism, British athletics and Coubertin's Olympism, but equally with the good party member unthinkingly and unquestionably committed to the cause and the community that is the Soviet Union.

Carl Lewis' victory in 1984 was equally convincing, but that is where similarities end. Throughout his career Lewis was a showman, an inveterate self-publicist, and almost oblivious to everyone around him except the crowd and the media. He was one of the first athletes to make a spectacle of himself: his performances were oriented towards increasing his recognition factor and star status. For Borzov, the elation of victory is momentarily signalled, then withdrawn; for Lewis it is the beginning of the show. As Lewis crosses the finishing line, he's already celebrating: he proceeds to skip and jump and gesticulate, pausing briefly en passant to almost shake hands with a teammate; then he runs to the crowd, covers himself in a huge American flag, and does a lap of victory. Nobody else matters: Lewis places himself in front of the television cameras, and commands their attention. There is nothing here that refers to self-discipline, restraint or any other value except the glory, status, capital and personal ecstasy that comes with winning.

The increased importance of the games as sites for demonstrating ideological or national value placed an even greater requirement on the athletic body to successfully stand in for and demonstrate the superiority of capitalism, communism or the nation; this led, indirectly, to the acceleration of professionalism and the use of performance enhancing drugs. As Moeller writes:

> The merging of political and commercial interests in sport created good growth conditions for . . . the use of doping . . . The typical example of politically determined doping misuse is the systematic doping of ignorant athletes in the former East Germany. The typical example of the correlation of commercial interests and doping problems is the temptingly large sums that companies are willing to pay for contracts to successful athletes. The best athletes can live a glamorous life whereas the less successful ones – if they are professional at all – are constantly threatened in their livelihood. (2004: 202)

The increased use of drugs and the changes to athletic bodies was to a large extent a consequence of the intensification of the Cold War competition being played out at the Olympics: drug taking was rife in the 1970s and 1980s, and only slowed down after improved testing regimes were introduced in 1989. Most of the current world records in women's sprinting dates from before 1989: athletes such as the East German Marita Koch and the American Florence Griffith-Joyner, for instance, achieved times that haven't been bettered over 20 years later (in the women's 400 and 100 metres, respectively) after quickly putting on significant muscle mass. Griffith-Joyner's bodily transformation, which she attributed to a regime of squats and weights, coincided with her improving her personal best in the 100 metres, at the US trials just before the Seoul games, to 10.49 seconds; the old world record was 10.76. In 1985 Koch ran the 400 metres in 47.6 seconds, breaking the old record by 0.4 of a second; since then no female athlete has run under 48 seconds.

During this period the bodies of female athletes became considerably more muscular, to an extent that it completely differentiated them, not just from female athletes of the 1960s, but even more dramatically from everyday female bodies. In the women's 400 metre final at the Tokyo games, won by the Australian Betty Cuthbert, the field was made up of bodies that were clearly exceptionally fit, but there was no pronounced muscle definition or development in the shoulders, the back, the legs, calves or buttocks; the only marker of their athletic status was that they were lithe, but not to the extent that their bodies would have been noticeable outside the athletic arena. In the women's sprint finals from 1980 to 1988 the athletes were exceptionally bigger and more powerful than non-athletes. It was not just a case of them being fitter, bigger, stronger and more muscular: they were the products of a physiological and biochemical regime entirely removed from the everyday.

To some extent this transformation of the female athletic sprinter's body during the 1980s can be explained in terms of women's athletics catching up with the level of professionalism found in men's sport, which involved much more sophisticated and intensive training regimes, and scientific and closely researched and monitored diets, exercise routines and use of weights. However, this argument fails to account for the fact that a similar dramatic transformation was taking place in male sprinters, the most infamous example being the Canadian Ben Johnson. Johnson broke the world record in winning the 100 metres at the 1988 games, but tested positive for an illegal substance three days later and was stripped of his gold medal. By the time of that race Johnson's body was almost grotesque in terms of its enhancements. All of the finalists in that race look preternaturally powerful, but Johnson is simply a ball of muscle bounding and bouncing away from all of them.

The Olympics as media spectacle

The 1936 Berlin Olympics had been notable as one of the first global media spectacles. Jonathan Crary has suggested that the spectacle, 'as Debord uses the term, probably does not effectively take shape until several decades into the twentieth century' (1998: 18); he cites the use of mass media techniques by the fascist government in Nazi Germany during the 1930s and 1940s as examples of this development. Television and audio-visual synchronization in film were concurrent with this development. Goebbels had pioneered the use of phonograph records, magazines and films during the German election of 1932, but the extent and coordination of media and other communication technologies used to promote the games while demonstrating the legitimacy and power of the Nazi Reich was not to be matched for several decades (Fest 1977: 473). By the mid-1930s Goebbels' propaganda committee:

> was providing 24,000 copies of its newsletter worldwide . . . This included 3,075 foreign newspapers and journals . . . the press service was enlarged and . . . translated in fourteen languages . . . Olympic placards were distributed complete with logo in nineteen languages and a total press run of 156,000 copies . . . leaflets were distributed in fourteen language and a press run of 2.4 million. The ten days of the torch run from Olympia to Berlin received the full attention of every aspect of the German media . . . in terms of participating journalists, these were by far the most successful games until 1964 . . . [with] 700 foreign journalists and 593 foreign media . . . 41 radio stations . . . reached an estimated 300 million radio listeners. (Kruger 2004: 44–5)

Scenes from the Berlin Olympics shown in Riefenstahl's film Olympiad articulate an ideological connection between the precision, power, grandeur and immensity of the event and the political regime of Nazism. Berlin offered spectacle without the celebrities; as with the Los Angeles Olympics of 1932, the technological and ideological preconditions for the contemporary version of the society of the spectacle are present in an incipient form, as is the focus on attention management and discourses of hyperbole. The Los Angeles and Berlin Olympics indicated the direction in which both the spectacle and the Olympic movement were heading in the second half of the twentieth century.

There are significant points of differentiation, however, between the Olympics-as-spectacle of the 1930s (both the totalitarian and democratic capitalist versions), and contemporary games. Fascism's use of the package of the mass media and sport to revive and naturalize ancient blood and race myths – Debord characterized it as 'a cult of the archaic completely fitted out by modern technology' – is clearly a 'factor in the formation of the modern spectacle' (2006: 77). For Debord, however, the society of the spectacle is ultimately about the replacement of society by various simulations produced by the commercial media. From this perspective, the Berlin-style spectacle, based on a cult of leadership and exclusivist and hard narratives, can be seen as something of a historical dead end, although it enjoyed an extended life of sorts in the Olympics games in Moscow in 1980, and again in Seoul in 1988.

The capitalist spectacle dominated in the post-Moscow Olympics period. Alan Tomlinson writes that the Los Angeles games' use of sponsorship, marketing and the media 'recast the Olympic mould', and constituted:

> a symbolic moment in the history of the modern Olympic Games, embodying its transformation in terms of media profile, marketing

opportunity and potential source of profit and personal aggrandizement for those purporting to live by the ideals of the Olympic movement. They were also the first Summer Games at which . . . Juan Antonio Samaranch . . . presided. His . . . capacity to strike exclusive deals with major multinationals and television companies . . . could be seen as the pivotal moment when the Olympics were steered down a path towards their Disneyfication. (2004: 148)

Los Angeles marked the moments when Olympism finally and moved irrevocably away from the discourse of Olympic sport as Coubertin had understood and articulated it. The production and reproduction of the games as a set of media texts oriented, packaged and edited so as to appeal to a series of specific demographics (most particularly the US television market), but also the widest possible part of each demographic (not just sports fans, but anyone who might be inclined to watch, and be held, by the hyperbole and manufactured drama, tension and nationalism), meant that television coverage took on a new form:

> For Montreal, ABC won with an offer of $25 million. With such sums at stake, ABC sports director, Roone Arledge, planned the coverage with the kind of detailed attention that coaches give to training schedules. 'We figured [Nadia] Comaneci would be big for us', he told *Sports Illustrated*'s Frank Deford . . . 'And in the second week, [Frank] Shorter is attractive enough to be big again . . . And Bruce Jenner . . . he's charismatic' . . . East Germany's Kornelia Ender, who was considered an unattractive commercial prospect, received scant notice from ABC . . . Track and field and swimming were extensively covered. The cameras lingered twice as long on the female as on the male gymnasts . . . Basketball fans had ninety minutes of their favourite sport, while most soccer fans probably missed the thirty five seconds devoted to the world's most popular game. (Guttmann 1992: 148)

The focus on entertainment also explains the transformation in, and the (televisual) significance now attached to, Olympic opening ceremonies. Ceremonies had constituted an important part of the ancient Olympics: but they were largely religious in character, and involved the taking of oaths and the performance of rituals of purification on the part of the competing athletes. Coubertin took his lead from Hellenism when, in an article published in the *Revue Olympique* in 1909, he outlined his ideas as to the most suitable form and style for ceremonies of the modern games. He suggested that they:

> should be short and simple. Only under those circumstances would the ceremony achieve the desirable sense of majesty. Any Olympia worthy of the name and its goals must give the . . . impression [of a] . . . sort of seriousness, not necessarily austere, but one that allows for joy . . .

so that, in the silence between competitions, it draws visitors as a place of pilgrimage, inspiring in them a respect for places devoted to noble memories and profound hopes. (Coubertin 2000: 256–7)

Coubertin insisted that Olympic ceremonies needed to demonstrate the religious sensibility that was germane to Greek athletics and games; they were not meant to be 'theatrical displays, useless spectacles incompatible with the seriousness and dignity of international athletic competitions' (580). He wrote later, in 1935, that in:

> response to my request, the games of the eleventh Olympiad will open to the incomparable sounds of the last movement of Beethoven's Ninth Symphony, sung by a powerful choral group . . . The harmony of the piece seemed to communicate with the divine. (583)

What was particularly pronounced in the Berlin ceremonies was the performance of an explicit socio-cultural narrative linking Hellenistic art and culture with the ethos and practices of contemporary sport. There was also another, underlying, discursive narrative in the accentuated racial characteristics of the Olympic statues; this was equally evident in Riefenstahl's film where ancient statues metamorphose into live discus and javelin throwers with recognizably Aryan features.

This use of the opening ceremony for the purposes of producing a visual discourse of the qualities and virtues of the host nation was taken up by subsequent host cities, although the hyperbole, intensity, drama and accompanying political metanarrative of Berlin was not really matched until the Cold War games of 1980 and 1984. This was largely a consequence of the tit-for-tat boycotts that up the ante, pitching totalitarian and capitalist spectacles against one another. The competition was played out in the stadiums and on television: in the opening ceremony of the Moscow games, 16 nations marched 'behind the Olympic rings or the ensign of their national Olympic committee, but none of these banners were shown on Soviet television' (Guttmann 1992: 155); what Guttmann neglects to add is that television commentary outside of the Soviet Union talked about little else. The Los Angeles opening ceremony was characterized by American jingoism, triumphalism and Hollywood excess: 84 grand pianos played Gershwin, and covered wagons carried brave pioneers across the plains (161), albeit without reprising the massacre or displacement of indigenous peoples.

Something of a similar discursive exchange was figured in the games held in Sydney, Athens and Beijing. One political context of Sydney being chosen to host the 2000 games was the surprise failure of the Beijing bid, apparently due to American opposition (Roche 2000: 156). In order to justify its choice, the organizers of the Sydney games went out of their way to emphasize goodwill, universalism and the ability of sport to overcome political, racial and cultural divisions. The indigenous athlete Cathy Freeman lit the Olympic flame, and when she won the Women's 400 metres sprint she pointedly carried both an Australian and an Aboriginal flag around the stadium. Unlike previous Olympic ceremonies, Sydney seemed to be intentionally distancing itself from the Hellenistic legacy; it produced instead a Rupert Murdoch inspired media spectacle that was as much about national pride and self-mythologizing as it was about sport. Athens in 2004 predictably returned 'with a vengeance' (Goff 2011: 13) to the Hellenistic motif, with a ceremony that echoed Riefenstahl's narrative of classicism begetting the modern, with representations of Cycladic heads, Minoan friezes, Pheidian statues, all acting out the Official Report's contention that 'the story of Greece leads the "journey of humankind from myth to logic"' (13). Beijing's ceremonies were an almost explicit retort to the favouring of Sydney's candidacy and a rebuttal of the occidental bias of Athens. Goff characterizes it as throwing:

> down a gauntlet to the western humanist tradition for which 'ancient Greece' remains a potent shorthand. Dramatising the invention of the printing press and the compass, as well as replaying epic Chinese voyages of discovery, Beijing 2008 seemed quite pointedly to demonstrate that some well-known contours of western civilisation are in fact eastern . . . Furthermore, the hallmark of the proceedings, spectacularly synchronised movements of immense masses of people, implicitly questioned the western obsession with the individual. (14)

Conclusion

The extent to which the discourse of spectacle has come to inhabit and supplant Olympism can be demonstrated by way of a description and analysis of Usain Bolt's performance before, during and after the 100 metres final at the 2012 London games. The first point worth noting is that athletes are now required to start their performance early: as he is announced, Bolt puts on his 'thunderbolt' pose, actively engages with the crowd and the television cameras, and crosses himself and points to the sky as he takes his mark. All the competitors in the final were more or less required to do something similar; and someone (presumably Bolt) has clearly 'coached' and advised Bolt's teammate and friend Yohan Blake to come up with his own distinctive performance of the 'claws and scowl of the beast'.

In the London final, the race was too tight for Bolt to start celebrating early, as he does in other races. However, once he passes the line, Bolt goes into a performance that is much more choreographed, organized and pointedly distinctive than anything Lewis ever did. The bodily hexis is all about the joy of victory – arms upraised, a wide, ecstatic smile, a vigorous acknowledgement of the crowd – but it also adheres to a carefully scripted routine. Bolt eventually drops to the ground, head bent and waits for the photographers to gather in front of him. Then he jumps to his feet, and gives the crowd and the media what they have been waiting for – the thunderbolt pose, which is the moment of assertion and triumph, but also his very distinctive brand mark.

Bolt is then surrounded by other athletes, including Blake, at which stage the routine becomes more routine: they pick up a Jamaican flag, and do a lap of victory together, occasionally going to and interacting with members of the crowd – friends, team members and Jamaican supporters. The race itself lasts less than 10 seconds, but the overall show – including post-race interviews and photography sessions – is continuous, to the extent that the schedule for presenting medals to the winners is sometimes altered because of the length and complexity of the celebrations. The imperative of putting on a spectacle for the media even interrupts the extent to which Bolt runs his races: if he's pressed, or if he's trying to break a record, then he runs himself out; otherwise an early signal to the crowd is likely, sometimes more than 20 metres from the finish line.

The media's coverage of Bolt's performance contains within it the salient features of the capitalist spectacle. First, everything is (potentially) reduced to the status of commodity, and there is an emphasis on necessary, repetitive and mobile (visual) consumption. Second and relatedly, attention is attracted and maintained because every moment of the coverage, every camera angle, close-up, slow motion shot and musical enhancement, offers – actually, demands – an affective identification and passionate response on the part of the audience. Third, the athletic contest as a specific cultural genre and discourse (a competition based on Hellenistic and English Athletics) is relegated to the status of an arbitrary content in an altogether hyperbolic and hysterical discursive apparatus that can only repeat itself to the effect that 'Everything that appears is good; what is good will appear' (Debord 2006: 15). As Bourdieu writes:

> What exactly do we mean when we talk about the Olympics? The apparent referent is what 'really' happens. That is to say, the gigantic spectacle of sport in which athletes from all over the world compete under the sign of universalistic ideals; as well as the markedly national, even patriotic ritual of the parades by various national teams, and the award ceremonies replete with flying flags and blaring anthems. But the hidden referent is the television show, the ensemble of representations of the first spectacle, as it is filmed and broadcast by television in selections which, since the competition is international, appear unmarked by national bias. The Olympics, then, are doubly hidden: no one sees all of it, and no one sees that they don't see it. Every television viewer can have the illusion of seeing the (real) Olympics. (2010: 62)

In our next two chapters we will look in more detail at the history of the relation between media genres and discourses and the field of sport, and specifically at how the discursive disjunct between the two fields has been played out within the practices and sites of popular sports such as football and cricket.

CHAPTER EIGHT

Television genres and sport

Introduction

This chapter is concerned with televisual sport; more specifically, it considers how television discourses, imperatives, genres and technologies have transformed sporting activities into something both other and more than itself. At a basic level and by way of exemplification, the simple division of sport into live and studio based sports genres and formats (a development that has only become a commonplace over the past 50 years) constitutes a significant extension of the field, producing and requiring new forms of analysis, knowledge, categories of expertise, modes of address and technologies of mediation – in both fields. Changes to and developments of the discourses and genres of televisual sport do more than simply contain or facilitate different sports contents; they produce meanings, narratives, ways of seeing and modes of spectatorship.

We argued that sport was originally located at what Bourdieu (1993) refers to as the autonomous pole of the field of cultural production, while the commercial media, which to large extent share the logics and imperatives of the field of business, are to be found at the opposite, heteronomous pole. Commercial television, for instance, is dominated by the twin constraints of 'time and effect' (Bourdieu 1998a). Bourdieu makes the point that even when television is covering important news stories, the very limited time available to present and explain the issues means that slogans, sensationalism and simplistic accounts are favoured over and stand in for complexities, contexts and histories. This makes it difficult for television to say anything much at all, which is why the news is invariably dominated by visuals. A 30-second description of a massacre, famine, riot or air strike can produce an immediate emotional effect. Audio-visual material of a person being beaten to death, emaciated babies, crowds destroying buildings, or of bombs zeroing in on bridges or enemy troops takes the viewer into the story, and can provoke an immediate and strong affective response (pity, anger, fear, revulsion, elation). This logic is accepted, complied with and naturalized across the field, which means that commercial media discourses and genres are largely carried over and reproduced when applied to sport. Consequently sports content is integrated into, and is experienced and seen through, the discourses, narratives, meanings and forms of address that characterize media genres.

Televisual genres are derived from, and produced in accordance with, this logic/economy of time and effect. Genre constitutes a particular form of discourse, and it carries out similar work. In John Frow's terms, genre functions as:

> a set of conventional and highly organised constraints on the production and interpretation of meaning . . . it's structuring effects guide, in a way that a builder's form gives shape to a pour of concrete, or a sculptor's mould shapes and gives structure to its materials. Generic structure both enables and restricts meanings, and is a basic condition for meaning to take place . . . No symbolically organised action takes place other than through the shaping of generic codes, where 'shaping' means both 'shaping by' and 'shaping of': acts and structures work upon and modify each other. (2006: 10)

In keeping with Frow's notion of generic framing as a dynamic and interactive process that simultaneously shapes and is shaped, this chapter will identify, explain and analyse how the content of sport has both been influenced and even transformed by, and to some extent has modified, the generic formats of the media. This line of inquiry is further contextualized by a consideration of the logics and imperatives of the relevant cultural fields – in this case sport and the media-as-business. To describe, analyse and understand the ways in which media formats and sport have influenced one another, we need to be aware of the field-specific contexts that have provided the impetus for the development of a relationship that is both well established (it dates back to the 1930s) but also something of a contemporary phenomenon (the sport–media nexus is really a post-1960s phenomenon).

Live television coverage of sport

There has been a close relationship between the field of sport and the print media since the latter part of the nineteenth century, and prior to the Second World War radio sports coverage played a significant role in both the United States and the United Kingdom (Guttmann 1986). This changed quickly in the United States: television attracted large audiences with its telecasts of boxing and college football in the 1940s and 1950s, and generally replaced radio to the extent that while the latter had been an 'essential part of daily life' in America in the 1930s, by the end of the 1940s 'the average American listened to the radio for only twenty four minutes a day' (134). In Britain the changeover was more gradual due to the well-established status and influence of BBC radio and the relatively slow development of a national transmitter system, but whereas in 'early 1950s less than 5% of households' possessed television sets, by the 1970s 'this was the proportion of those that did not' (Hill 2002: 103).

The genre that most helped to sell the television–sport nexus to a wide demographic in Britain and America was the live outdoor coverage, particularly of popular events such as football games, boxing matches and horse racing meetings (Boyle and Haynes 2000; Hill 2002; Holt 1989). Live sporting telecasts have their own particular discourses, characteristics and forms of address predicated on the imperative to simulate, as closely as possible, the 'feel' of being at the game. Initially the limitations of the technology of the 1930s, 1940s and 1950s made live television sport a poor substitute for the real thing, since 'cameras were fixed and were fitted with lenses that made the performers appear as tiny figures' (Cashmore 1990: 144). Referring to technical problems encountered in the BBC's televising of a rugby international between England and Scotland in 1938, and more specifically in the mismatch between the visual text and the authentic experience of live, at the ground spectators, Boyle and Haynes explain that:

> the positioning of the cameras was clearly viewed as the optimum use of the telephoto lenses to capture the play in each third of the field. The sheer bulkiness of the technology required to transmit for sport, specifically the mass of cable involved, severely restricted the mobility of the equipment. The problem of economically marshalling the technology needed on location took many years to resolve. (2000: 41)

However, by the 1960s techniques and technology had improved, equipment had become more mobile, and the live televisual text was now:

> able to combine documentary accuracy with a fast tension worthy of the most thrill-packed sports occasions. The high-gloss presentations had analyses of slow-motion replays and frozen moments, knowledgeable commentaries-cum-evaluations, and detailed close-ups that captured facial – and sometimes verbal – expressions that the attending fans could never pick up. Around the event, TV learned to edit events down to lean action and pad events with previews, postscripts, and all manner of factual information, all designed to make viewing from home a more enriching experience. (Cashmore 1990: 144–5)

The major changes to live sports broadcast occurred in the United States in the 1960s were based on satisfying two imperatives that were central to the commercial television: first, appeal to the widest demographic in order to maximize revenue; and second, and by way of facilitating the first imperative, hyperbolize everything so that it becomes more dramatic, spectacular and attention grabbing. The first significant attempt to achieve these aims came about when American television sports producer Roone Arledge introduced a number of innovations to television sport including slow motion replays; split screens; half-time analysis and highlights; hand-held close-up shots; situational cameras and microphones; cameras and microphones directed at the crowd to help build a sense of atmosphere; tightly edited packages that increased suspense and eliminated 'slow' play; opinionated 'personalities' as announcers; and Monday Night Football and the 'Wide World of Sports' program. Television had 'been content to bring the viewer the game' (Roberts and Olson 1997: 418) by using a small number of static cameras. This was enough 'for those who loved football, but it was not very attractive to the casual viewer' (418) who had:

> one eye on the screen and one hand on the dial . . . Arledge wrote: 'What we set out to do was to get the audience involved emotionally. If they didn't give a damn about the game, they still might enjoy the program.' To do this Arledge used more cameras. He put cameras on cranes and blimps and helicopters to provide a better view of the stadium, the campus, and the town. His technicians developed hand-held cameras for close-ups. In the stadium he employed seven cameras, three just for capturing the environment. 'We asked ourselves: If you were sitting in the stadium, what would you be looking at? The coach on the sideline, the substitute quarterback warming up, the pretty girl in the next section. So our camera wandered as your eyes would.' Often what Arledge decided would interest his mostly male viewers were young and beautiful women . . . The game was only one part of the sporting experience. (418)

The use of technologies and techniques that took audiences 'to the game', along with changes to rules that were designed to make professional sport attractive to a wider demographic, necessarily brought live sport coverage closer to logics and the discourses of the spectacle. However, sporting events rarely keep viewers closely attentive or interested for a protracted period: an NFL game might be too one-sided and therefore dead as a contest by half-time, or a football match may drag on towards a dull scoreless draw because neither side is prepared to risk losing. When nothing is happening in televised sport, commentators need to produce something in its place – discourses that reflected or invoked soap-like passion, drama, scandal, rivalry, heroism, dreams, sex, celebrities, ambition, betrayal, power struggles and intrigue.

Commercial television was committed to increasing the demographic of its sports audience, which meant attracting and holding the attention of new viewers who were often unfamiliar with sports rules and traditions, and illiterate and/or indifferent with regard to skills. Consequently, they exercised a considerable influence both over media coverage of sport and the way games were played. If this viewer was unsure whether, in Bourdieu's (2000) terms, the game was 'worth the candle', it was very much up to the media and sports administrators to ensure that it was – if only because being (even vaguely or ephemerally) attentive to the sports event provided television ratings and potential audiences for advertising. Consequently televised sport is now watched by an increasing number of casual spectators who 'see only violence and confusion' (Bourdieu 1991: 364). As Pierre Bourdieu writes, one only has to think of what is implied:

> in the fact that a sport like rugby (in France – but the same is true of American football in the USA) has become, through television, a mass spectacle, transmitted far beyond the circle of present or past 'practitioners' . . . to a public very imperfectly equipped with the specific competence needed to decipher it adequately. The 'connoisseur' has schemes of perception and appreciation which enables him to see what the layman cannot see, to perceive a necessity where the outsider sees only violence and confusion, and so to find in the promptness of a movement, in the unforeseeable inevitability of a successful combination or the near-miraculous orchestration of a team strategy, a pleasure no less intense and learned than the pleasure a music-lover derives from the particularly successful rendering of a favourite work. The more superficial the perception, the less it finds its pleasure in the spectacle contemplated in itself and for itself, and the more it is drawn to the search for the 'sensational'. (364)

This kind of bifurcation has characterized the relation between live television coverage and, for instance, the sport of cricket. Commercial and television-driven imperatives have effectively led to both the live coverage and the game itself splitting into different generic forms: these are along the lines of the traditional version, played over three or five days (for test matches), and the more recent one-day and twenty–twenty games, which are concluded within 8 and 3 hours, respectively. The live coverage of test matches reflects the pace, decorum and seriousness – the history-as-gravitas – of the game, whether it is on English, Australian, Indian, Caribbean or South African television. The technical changes and additions – such as cameras behind the bowlers at both ends, multiple cameras around the boundary, stump- and sky-cam, bowling speed readouts, and simulated reproductions and projections of bowling line, length, height and direction – have not transformed the style and pace of the coverage, or the way in which that coverage discursively and visually addresses the audience. Talking heads chat politely among themselves, provide a technical report on the state of the pitch, and do not become agitated or apologetic, or slip into the sensational, if there isn't a lot of immediate action. They presume that the audience is able to understand and appreciate that because the game is spread over five days, significance and excitement will build gradually, and that there will be interest and even entertainment at the level of minutiae (a ball carefully defended, the flight achieved by a slow bowler). Live televisual test cricket is not only watched by Bourdieu's connoisseurs: the audience, regardless of their level of literacy, are addressed as if they were connoisseurs, or connoisseurs in training; in other words, the commentary, visuals, information provided and forms of address – the parts that together constitute and characterize the discourse – are commensurate with the way in which test cricket discursively articulates the relationship between itself and its audience.

While the technical aspects of live television coverage of cricket have been refined and developed since the 1970s, the most significant changes to the approaches and imperatives of the genre are to be found in coverage of one-day and twenty–twenty games. The supposed innovations that characterized the 'Packer revolution' of the 1970s (see Cashmore 1990; Hill 2002; Holt 1989), such as bringing in coloured clothing, stump-cameras, white balls, floodlit games, cameras at both ends of the ground and pitch-metres) were lauded for making a traditional, complex, nuanced and slow game more dramatic, interesting, relevant and involving for a generalist audience; in fact, they simply brought in variations on discourses, techniques, technologies and forms of address that had been in use in television coverage of American college, NFL and NBA games for almost two decades. Even a recent development such as sky-cam – used in the NFL and Australian rules to produce the effect of a soaring and swooping bird's-eye view of the action – is just an extension of Ardledge's technology-driven attempt to make sport 'more than itself'.

One-day internationals, which date from the 1970s, are a good example of the transformation of a game in order to suit television. Unlike test cricket, one-day games are played both day and night, team wear coloured clothing, the duration of the game is limited to approximately 8 hours (and played at times that specifically fit in with the imperatives of television scheduling) and there are additional rules regarding the kind of deliveries that are legitimate, and fielding positions (which ensures that matches are livelier and more interesting to laymen). Twenty–twenty cricket is a more frenetic version of the one-day game (with innovations such as 'supersubs'), and has only been played on a regular basis since the new millennium. It is designed almost exclusively to fit in with television schedules and requirements: games last a couple of hours, and players are wired and respond to questions from commentators as the game is being played.

One-day and twenty–twenty cricket games are often abhorred and avoided by traditionalists, but attract larger crowds and much higher television ratings; the changes that have been developed in the format mirror the wider, younger, less cricket literate demographic that make up a large part of their audience. The most extreme and recent example of this development can be found in the Twenty–Twenty Indian Premier League (IPL) Cricket competition, which was designed primarily for live television; tickets are given away in their thousands in order to ensure a lively and visible crowd. The competition was created by the Board of Control for Cricket in India (BCCI), and television rights were secured by India's Sony Entertainment Television Network and Singapore's World Sport Group, with regional broadcasting rights being shared by networks in Australia, Britain, the Arab Gulf states, North America, South Africa, Pakistan and across Asia (see www.iplcricketforum.com). The format is part Bollywood film, part Entertainment Network (Indian style), with a very quick game of cricket sharing time with the dancing girls (and boys) and celebrities. At one game a prominent Bollywood star was refused entry to the team dugout to watch the game, so the league promptly changed the rules to allow this commingling of celebrities and sport.

The discursive differences that characterize media coverage of the different forms of cricket were on show during an incident that occurred in a one-day international match between England and New Zealand, played on 26 June 2008. A New Zealand player (Grant Elliot) was going for a run when he bumped into the English bowler Ryan Sidebottom, and was knocked to the ground and run out. The spirit of the game dictates that the fielding captain (Paul Collingwood) should withdraw the appeal – Elliot was impeded, and it would be considered the worst of bad form to maintain the appeal. Collingwood, however, refused to withdraw. This created an extraordinary furore – the New Zealand players gestured angrily from their changing rooms, the crowd jeered loudly, and journalists started writing about it in dramatic and slightly hysterical terms (would it be the end of Collingwood's career, had cricket lost its soul). In the middle of all this the television commentators (a collection of former cricket captains and other distinguished now-retired players) simply went on covering the game as if nothing much had happened; they didn't think (or were acting and speaking as if they didn't think) the incident was of sufficient importance to become the sole focus of attention. The one commentator who did try to run with and hyperbolize the incident – the ex-New Zealander wicketkeeper Ian Smith – was quickly 'put in his place'. In this instance, there was a refusal of the imperative to take the game too far from the values, practices and meanings of the field.

As we suggested earlier, the IPL and its television coverage have certainly moved cricket 'elsewhere' – more or less into the world of Bollywood films and the Entertainment channel, with dancing and singing frequently punctuating the action; film and television soap stars rubbing shoulders with, and taking the spotlight from, players; and huge amounts of money becoming the focus of attention (how much will teams bid for Shane

Warne, who will win the prize for the most sixes). In test and to some extent ODI cricket, on the other hand, the live genre, along with its foci and modes of address, has by and large acceded to the 'sport-as-ethos, without regard to, or perhaps simply disdainful of, the imperative to hystericize and hyperbolize everything.

Developments such as the IPL are symptomatic of the radical transformation of the live television sport coverage format, and not just with regard to cricket. Virtually all live television sport – the NFL in the United States, AFL in Australia, football in Italy, Brazil and Japan – are now tied in to servicing wider demographics. Changes to the genre have also changed how games are seen and experienced. Viewers watching live television coverage of an NFL game are meant to be overwhelmed by, and caught up in, the build-up to the event. This is brought about in a number of ways. First, the upcoming game will be advertised, to saturation level, at least a week before the event takes place, usually by emphasizing the significance of the game, which may be predicated on standings ('the battle for first place'), the quality of the participants ('two undefeated teams'), or the status, achievements and rivalries of some of the protagonists ('Eli and Peyton Manning go head to head'; 'Tom Brady is poised to break Dan Marino's touchdowns record'). The advertisement will be accompanied by loud music and a frenetic race through clips of one team scoring, violent collisions and confrontations, superhuman bodies, players displaying extraordinary athleticism and skill (a spectacular quarterback pass and a diving reception), scantily clad cheer squads dancing, and colourfully dressed and outfitted fans celebrating or in despair. The particular event is represented as both larger than life (for instance, the passion of players and spectators is beyond the ordinary and everyday) and unceasingly exciting. Players will be shown in a manner that emphasizes their iconic status (a close-up of a veteran) or their imposing physicality (huge linemen shown, filmed up close and from below so that they seem to tower over the viewer). Moreover, the content, brevity and speed of the clips (in two senses: one scene quickly replaces another, and the action is often sped up) effectively work to guarantee that the game will be exciting.

Television advertisements of upcoming sporting events – a subgenre in its own right – work to get the attention of viewers, but it also disposes and creates expectations: it is then up to the commentary team, and the techniques and technologies they bring to the coverage (camera angles, points of emphasis, what's shown in replays) to do everything they can to help meet these expectations because the game itself will almost inevitably fall short of what has been promised. Even the most exciting game will have periods when nothing much is happening. Commentators can always go back to and analyse significant plays and developments, or project towards upcoming moments of excitement and drama; but the absence of immediate drama remains a threat to the maintenance of viewer interest and attention.

There are various techniques that commentators and directors use to overcome this challenge. Directors have numerous camera angles, close-ups, flying shots, blimp views and freeze frames from which to choose: there are usually enough available visuals that are sufficiently personal (the close-up of a coach's passion-filled face); disturbing (the sight and sound of a safety flying into a vulnerable wide receiver); dramatic (the shot of a huge and imposing defensive line defending waiting to repel a running back from their 1-yard line); or aesthetic (the city lights at night, skaters on a nearby frozen river) to arrest and maintain viewer interest and attention for long stretches of a game, without the need for verbal hyperbole.

Hyperbole, however, is always an important standby. The fact that the upcoming play in an NFL game is a relatively insignificant third (down) and 17 (yards to get the next down) in a quiet phase of the game, perhaps just before half-time with little chance of a score, can and often needs to be transformed into a crucial moment for the quarterback, whose confidence and subsequent performance suddenly depends on him completing this throw; or there is a reference to the psychological blow this will deal to the defending team, who will be thrown into disarray and disorganization if they succumb. Making too much of nothing wears thin very quickly, however. The next steps are to show replays of exciting plays that happened earlier; speculate about whether an important player is carrying an injury; show (from numerous angles) and analyse a contentious refereeing ruling that 'may be crucial'; introduce a personal element by panning to a rookie running backs' parents sitting proudly in the crowd; or if there is somebody sufficiently newsworthy, iconic or outstanding, concentrate the cameras and the commentary on that player ('Is this the last time we'll have the privilege of watching Peyton Manning on Monday Night football?').

If a game is boring and uneventful, outdoor telecasts sometimes make use of a strategy that strongly characterizes studio sport programs, where the hosts act as 'personalities' who provide much of the entertainment (by arguing with each other, articulating passionate opinions and beliefs, playing the buffoon): in the absence of drama, excitement or interest, commentators have to become the show. This is what often happens on Monday NFL, which promoted itself through reference to, and frequently makes use of, recognizable, avuncular, much respected or strongly opinionated former players or coaches (as it did with John Madden). Other telecasts have panels of commentators, usually made up of prominent ex-players, who are not particularly acute or analytical but provide a passable line of comic banter. If none of this works and all the normal avenues have been exhausted, the commentators may revert to a slightly more dangerous form of hyperbole, which is to represent and characterize the game as outstandingly boring, stupefyingly uninteresting, egregiously dull: in this way the commentators hope to turn negative capital into something above and beyond the everyday, and therefore perversely interesting.

Studio sport

Live sport telecasts offers the prospect of spontaneous excitement, passion and drama, so gaining a viewer's attention can be straightforward enough; on the other hand it is clearly a difficult proposition to maintain that attention, precisely because there's no way to control the script. The studio sport show format doesn't face that problem: while it may share the content of live sport telecasts, it has more obvious affinities with other television genres such as the news, current affairs, variety and chat shows. The comparison with the news format is based on similarities with regard to how time and material is organized and structured, the function of visuals, the forms of address employed, the role and tenor of presenters, and the perceived audiences. Sport news shows are usually fronted by middle-aged men whose main role is to perform smoothness, professionalism and reliability: like mainstream news readers, they need to look, act and speak as if they are trustworthy, and know what they are talking about. In order to appeal to a wider demographic, women presenters are becoming more prevalent, but they still constitute something of an exception to the all-male rule that has dominated televised sport since its inception.

Stories are arranged, and time allocated, in terms of perceived significance and topicality, although shows on channels that telecast a particular sport are likely to focus on upcoming games; in other words, some stories simultaneously function as news reports and advertisements. The imperative to perform reliability and professionalism means that verbal hyperbole is often limited in comparison with live telecasts; and because of time constraints visuals are more modestly employed, either to show action from recently completed games (a winning touchdown, a record breaking reception), particularly spectacular action (a length of the field punt return), or simply to serve as 'pieces of the real' (a story about a player or team not in action recently usually features representative archival footage). This ties in with the expectation that audiences are more likely to consist of both connoisseurs and laymen: sport news is not directed predominantly at those with a fleeting and fashionable attachment to the field, but at long-term fans who have an interest in what is happening to their team or sport. Gaining and holding attention is much less an issue here: the sports fan is likely to remain viewing once the scandalous and the spectacular have given way to the minutia of team tactics and rule changes.

While television sport genres are largely directed at sport connoisseurs, shows and audiences are likely to be split along the lines of class, profession and level of education. One generic form resembles current affairs programs, with relatively sophisticated, informed and extended discussions and interviews: the discourse is considered and restrained rather than hyperbolic; visuals are employed as a means of furthering analysis, rather than as a spectacular end-in-themselves; and attention is presumed, rather than something continually at risk. This genre is to be found predominantly but not exclusively in European countries (in a sense they are the televisual equivalent of the traditional serious sporting print press as represented by *L'Equipe*, *France Football* and *Gazetta del Sport*). A second generic form shares a number of features with variety, quiz and talk shows, and is best described as sports entertainment: interviews are often loud, jovial and disrespectful; comments intentionally outrageous and hyperbolic; and visuals geared towards the eccentric, weird, comic and the sexual (gratuitous clips of inadvertent collisions; egregious mistakes and embarrassing moments; scantily clad spectators and cheerleaders; and streakers). These shows, which are found extensively in the British Commonwealth (the United Kingdom, Australia and New Zealand), find their print precursors in English 'lads' magazines and tabloid press.

It is important to emphasize that the genres described here do not always manifest themselves in accordance with, or strictly adhere to, any formulae, categories or characteristics: television genres have always found room for hybridity, and television sport is no exception. The ESPN network, for instance, runs conventional sport news and documentary formats, but it also has shows which concentrate on American sport (baseball, NFL, college football) and presume an audience of connoisseurs – who want to be entertained. So discussions may start off as informed and literate, but they often degenerate into abuse, comedy and hyperbole; topics are covered in a few minutes or seconds; there is more emphasis placed on wit than there is on analysis; the participants (sports broadcasters and journalists) push themselves, their opinions and prejudices, to the fore; and visuals are used as the departure point for arguments rather than analysis. The issue of attention is once again central, but it is addressed and maintained by the production of an almost hysterical relation to the subject matter: comments, analysis, discussions and arguments are intense and intensive, but they always presage flight to another topic or issue.

Conclusion

Television coverage has influenced, inflected and changed the field of sport in a variety of ways: certain games, or forms of games, have arisen, come into prominence or been privileged over others; rules and playing conditions have been altered to make a sport more television-friendly; the size of television markets often determines where teams are located. Once this close relationship between television and sport developed, it fed back into and influenced the field in a number of ways. At a very basic level, television more or less picked up and tied itself to certain sports and events and ignored others. In Britain the excitement generated by live television coverage of football and the Five/Six Nations rugby competition simply reinforced their mass audiences and high media profiles. In those cases, capital simply attracted capital: demographics widened; sponsorship, advertising and broadcast rights revenue poured in; and salaries and prize-money increased. Some low-profile sports benefited from the advent of television, precisely because the pace and content of the games were highly suited either to taking spectators into the action, or because they allow for a close association between televisual images and commentary – both important components of the live coverage format. In the United Kingdom, snooker and darts benefited because they are relatively static and small-space activities. Cameras can follow the action easily while also focusing intimately on the face and expressions of the players and the reactions of the crowd, and the commentators have time to presage, narrate and 'build up' every shot or throw. In the United States and elsewhere poker has become a major 'sport' because the scenario of a small number of players packed into a room, sitting adjacent to and continually reacting with one another, is perfect for creating and showing tension, suspense, drama and passion, and promoting larger-than-life or eccentric characters: in other words, it is well suited to live television.

Sports such as squash, table tennis, badminton, sailing and athletic field events, on the other hand, have suffered precisely because they are not television-friendly. Squash, for instance, is both architecturally unsuitable (players could come between the ball and cameras placed behind or above the action), as well as being simply too fast for viewers to follow, or for commentators to do much more than 'talk across' the action. Most tellingly, a great deal of time can be expended in a rally where the players hit the ball up and down the wall waiting for a mistake – and it may take a long time to not happen. Contrast this with an NFL game, where each play can be anticipated, explained, analysed, evaluated, contextualized (by the main commentators, special comments person, sideline reporters) and broken down into multi-angled slow motion 'slices', and where the frequency of time-outs and changes of possession allows for the insertion of numerous commercial breaks. Faced with declining participation numbers and revenue, squash officials have done everything to revamp the game for television, including introducing fluorescent balls and transparent walls and changing the scoring system, but nothing has really worked. Without live television coverage the chances of squash receiving attention in studio sport are considerably reduced, which has meant that it has become a predominantly participatory, rather than a spectator, sport.

Television (and by extension the public relations and marketing industries) has taken on the task of promoting and commoditizing sport and sports consumption to global audiences. To some extent this simply involves promoting sport to lucrative non-traditional sport markets (popularizing men's soccer in the United States, rugby in Japan, the NFL in Europe, tennis and golf in China), as well as targeting groups based on gender (attracting women to more male dominated sports such as rugby), ethnicity (raising the profile of Australian rules football within migrant communities in Australia), class (promoting cricket and rugby to a working-class demographic in the United Kingdom) and age (making bowls, ten pin bowling and golf more appealing and relevant to younger audiences in the United States). The contemporary field of sport initially characterized, and continues to articulate, itself as relatively autonomous – seemingly at odds with, and above and beyond, the more commercially driven fields of the media, entertainment and business. And yet the history of sport in the twentieth century shows that the cultural field, or amalgam of fields, that most influenced sport is media-as-business; and the textual and institutional sites that most frequently manifest and reproduce this influence are those of television. The history of this relationship, most specifically between sport and television genres and their forms of address, is an ongoing set of negotiations that neither side can afford to lose – or win.

CHAPTER NINE

Media interactivity and fantasy sport

Introduction

The sport–media nexus has been the most significant factor in the transformation of the field of sport and its discourses and practices: it has effectively redefined how spectators see and experience games, and indeed what we understand by the notion of spectatorship. Many sports audiences, supporters and spectators now experience professional sport exclusively via television, newspapers, magazines and new media (the internet, digital phones) coverage. The use of technologies and techniques that take you 'into the game', along with changes to rules that are designed to make professional sport attractive to wider media demographics, has produced a situation where professional sport is now very much accessed and experienced through, and understood and engaged with in terms of, the perspectives, logics, imperatives and technologies – the ways of seeing – of the media. The desire to maximize these mediatized sports audiences has gone hand in hand with the development of strategies that seek to commoditize sport in a more detailed, lucrative and intensive manner. The most important of these developments are the interactive dimension of media sports coverage and fantasy sport.

Interactivity and sport

Media interactivity in the field of sport functions as both a lure and a way of transforming a viewer's relation to a game. At a basic level it brings audiences into the sports media mix. So on the BBC Sport website, for example, there is a 'Have your say' facility (recently updated to a page called '606'), a boxed section which allows fans to offer brief general comments on contemporary sports events and issues; there is a live update of scores and incidents from the European Champions League and international games interpolates television viewer's predictions and reactions; from these facilities there is a link to a site where, while a game is in progress, those same fans can rank and evaluate (by providing a score of 1 to 10) player performances. The comments are necessarily inane and the content irrelevant: the point is that the viewer is now (a very insignificant and temporary) part of the story.

The BBC Sport website shows the extent to which major sport websites have taken on the pedagogical task of acquainting a mass audience with a variety of sports and their rules, skills, histories and cultures, and by extension turning them into sport fans and consumers; this is very much akin to what happened with newspapers in the early part of the twentieth century. Interactivity serves this purpose by turning the viewer as consumer into part of the text that is being consumed. The fact that the game is taking place is not enough; the response of the fans must be inscribed into the logic of the spectacle, even if that response functions as a tautological assertion of the fans' presence. As a European Champions League game is updated play by play ('Shot by Ronaldo on Milan goal high and wide right'), the fans comments are not just integrated into the information stream as forms of evaluation/commentary ('United getting on top'; 'We need to make more of these chances'), but initiate dialogues and threads that generate their own mini audiences and participants, with topics of conversation that are usually, but not necessarily, tied to the game at hand.

This development is not specific to the BBC site. The Australian Football League (AFL) website 'Bigfooty' provides forums for fans of the teams, where participants produce threads on issues such as team selections, trade news, injuries, club politics and anything else of relevance, as well as posting photographs and clips (of match highlights, interviews and occasionally brawls). There is also a page for discussing/commenting on games as they happen, involving both sets of fans. If a match is particularly close, or informed by dramatic changes in the score, then that will tend to be the focus of comments. However, and as is the case with all mediated sporting contests, games can go through very dull periods, with the likelihood of a loss of audience interest. This is the main attraction and advantage of interactivity as an incitement to, and a form of, (self-)consumption: watching oneself and other fans as correspondents in action – as part of the game, and more generally the media – takes up the slack when the game fails to deliver or generate excitement, or elicit passion.

At an initial level the participants will introduce themselves, briefly ('I'm Buddy, a Hawk's fan'), ask questions ('Is Mitchell injured?'); provide information often derived from the still privileged position of watching television coverage of the game ('Starting to rain'); and boast about their team or disparage opponents. But more often than not forms of involvement and comments take on a life of their own, sometimes tending towards the ludic: too many undifferentiated or naïve questions about the absence of a particular player or the state of the game, for instance, will produce mock versions and responses that continue throughout the game, almost as a parody of the 'chant and response' activities of live crowds at British football games. This is analogous to the situation with talkback radio, where the listener's reactions and opinions are given a public voice and airing; but it also mirrors the (inter)activity of events such as the Wellington (New Zealand) Rugby Sevens competition, which attracts large crowds composed mainly of people who dress up and perform in an over the top manner (men as nurses, grown women as schoolgirls) – specifically for the amusement and entertainment of television cameras and their audiences. The unwritten contract that underlies the crowd's involvement is that of a requirement to perform for the television cameras and viewers. During the tournament, the spectators in the stadium have no expectation and no means to pay attention to results, the tabulation of scores into pool standings, or the progression through quarter finals, semifinals and finals of the three parallel competitions (bowl, plate, cup). This information is rarely posted even on the giant screens, and nobody seems to care too much.

An interactive dimension of some kind is now a necessary aspect of every major sport website, and in the most popular sites the level of interactivity is becoming both more pervasive and sophisticated. The BBC Sport website initially had one link on its home page where correspondents could send in to the point one liners about the event of the moment or day ('Sack the coach', 'Chelsea players are a disgrace'). But as the relatively basic mix of scores, reports and analysis has now burgeoned to include pages with photographs, tips and tactics tutorials, parodies, dietary advice, health and fitness programs, celebrity diaries, blogs, movable line-up predictors, gossip/rumours and audio-visual clips (the latest goals, violent incidents, how to improve your butterfly stroke), most of which have an interactive facility (rate this article on a scale of 1 to 5, provide your own tips and advice).

This interactive facility is also becoming part of other forms of media sports coverage. The UK BSkyB's digital service, for instance, allows viewers to choose their own camera angles and frames, and split the screen to display different games or to show a sporting event and the various betting odds available. As an English Premier League game is being played, viewers can edit the coverage in real time. In breaking down each minute or aspect of play, the spectator is thoroughly and pervasively integrated into what we could describe, following Baudrillard, as 'a world of generalized hysteria' characterized by a 'flight from one signifier to another' (2003: 77). The BSkyB facility produces a hystericized form of watching albeit in a very focused and detailed way: the viewer uses the available technology and her/his presumed literacy to break the game down into signs and sites of consumption (moments, angles, frames, patterns and tendencies) with the promise of returns (the pleasure of knowing, finding and predicting).

Fantasy sport

The lure of interactivity is perhaps even more germane to fantasy sport, to the extent that it produces new sets of relations between spectators as fans and sporting contests, and to a large extent transforms the visual regime of sport spectatorship. Fantasy sport started in the United States, either 40 (Shipman 2005) or just under 30 years ago (Isidore 2003), depending on the criteria you privilege; earlier leagues were small and private, later leagues larger and more public, and were often located in and played through newspapers. The first leagues started with 'owners compiling weekly stats with various sports newspapers, such as the Sporting News' (Isidore 2003). Competitions moved quickly to, and are now played mainly on, the internet: it had the advantage of being able to provide services 'that would quickly crunch the stats and send out standings via email or post them on a Web site', which gave the games 'explosive double digit growth through most of the 1990s' (Isidore 2003). This initial level of growth has been maintained: a study conducted in 1999 estimated that in the United States almost 30 million people aged 18 and over played some form of fantasy sport, which translated to 15 per cent of that particular demographic (Zillgitt 2000). Although the earliest games were started by baseball fans, currently the most popular fantasy sport is the National Football League (NFL) with '93% of fantasy players participating . . . More than 60% play fantasy baseball, while other sports account for 30% of the market or less' (Woodward 2004).

Fantasy players process all the available information and statistics and function as virtual managers who draft actual players, or bid for them in auctions, and form virtual squads/teams that usually replicate real numbers and positions (an ice hockey team based on the NHL will have centres, wingers, goalkeepers and defenders). The leagues then take the statistics from NHL games (goals, assists) and transpose those to fantasy league games. While the Ottawa Senators are beating the Edmonton Oilers by five goals to three, the statistics generated by that game are being used (often immediately) in thousands of fantasy leagues to determine results. Many leagues are hosted by the sports section of large internet news sites (Yahoo, USA Today, Fox, CBS), although an increasing number are run by private providers as businesses. Fantasy sport attract up to 30 million players in America alone (Shipman 2005: 2), and they are served by an increasing number of specialist magazines, television sports shows and internet file providers who give advice on who to draft or pick up from the waiver wire, track injuries and statistical variations, and rank players week to week according to their fantasy (rather than their actual) value. In fantasy leagues virtually every aspect of a particular sport is potentially available, and is produced, as a site of significance. Providers such as Yahoo have default settings to which most public leagues adhere: a public ice hockey (NHL based) league, for instance, will make use of obvious categories such as goal scoring and assisting, as well as reasonably cognate or logically derived variations such as a player's plus/minus rating (based on whether their team scored or conceded goals while they were on the ice), power play or short-handed points (goals and assists achieved with a numerical advantage or disadvantage), game winning goals and shots on goal. However, they also include not so obvious categories such as penalties in minutes (PIMs). When a player receives a 2-minute penalty, say, he hands the opposition a considerable advantage (they are playing with an extra man for that period), so it makes sense that taking a penalty would constitute a negative score – but in most NHL based fantasy leagues acquiring PIMs is a positive category. A fantasy sport participant watching or following a game can sometimes be completely oblivious to who is winning, or which players are playing well or scoring goals: instead they may be focused on animosities between players that could lead not just to minor infractions (tripping, high sticking), but to violent confrontations that will earn a player a 5-or 10-minute penalty. Those penalties are translated into positive points for the fantasy game players. The production of game statistics that is inherent to the appreciation of sports have been translated into parallel scoring systems and the manufacturing of results which bare no immediate relation to the sanctioned games' outcomes.

This process has a strong temporal dimension, as well: fantasy managers follow the minutia associated with players, games and competitions over the course of the season, sometimes throughout most of the day, every day. In leagues based on sports that only play two or three days a week, such as the NFL, the English Premier League or Australian Rules, the focus is relatively condensed and therefore particularly intense. During the NFL season on a Sunday (US time) fantasy managers can shift back and forth from television sets to computers following and taking in different developments and information (touchdowns, field goals, yards gained by running backs, quarterback pass completions, tackles and sacks recorded by individual defensive players, injuries, changes to the state of the game which necessitate the quarterback on one team to throw at all cost), and this will be drawn out from the first kickoff (at 1 p.m. eastern US time) until the end of the last game that night (Pacific time). In leagues based on sports that are played most days (NHL, MLB) the level of frenetic intensity is not so much reduced as extended and subject to rhythms of intensity. There are days when all teams play, such as Saturday with MLB and Thursday and Saturday with the NHL. But even on days when there are only a few games being played (Sunday in the NHL, say) the significance of a particular category of scoring, and hence the level of intensity of focus and involvement, will fluctuate depending on the state of play in the fantasy competition: the real game may be decided by half-time, and consequently of little interest to conventional ice hockey fans and spectators; but to numerous fantasy players any development (a meaningless goal or penalty incurred) or even non-development (no goals would mean a shut-out for a goalkeeper) is potentially vital.

While games, and the statistics they produce, constitute the prime concern of fantasy players, their extended temporal involvement and focus is not actually dependent on whether or not games are being played. Fantasy sport never rests: there are always texts, sites, information, news, trends, rumours, rankings, statistics, discussions, lists, trades and other activities, resources and developments to consider. The Yahoo sport site has a fantasy section which links to five different NFL based games; major fantasy games based on college football, the NBA, the NHL and the MLB, and less utilized games involving sports such as golf and car racing. The general fantasy page provides links to generic articles and sites, updated daily, pertinent to each fantasy game. For the NFL based games there are articles on the best free agent/waiver wire pickups (players still available in most leagues), advice about who to trade away and trade for and what to offer, which underperforming players are likely to improve, who to start and bench each week (depending on matchups); and lists and rankings of players both generally (the top 50 or 100 players) and by position (for instance, the top 20 running backs each week).

League home pages provide information about the teams involved, their managers, progress scores and tables (which will vary depending on whether the league uses a rotisserie or head to head format), schedules, which players were drafted in what order, current rosters, recent transactions, messages ('smack' talk or boasting, exchanges, debates, suggestions), and more links to expert advice and information (injuries, competition for positions, 'stock market' fluctuations, scouting reports, statistics about player involvement). There are also a link to each team's own page (which contains a record of the players on the roster, upcoming games, past results and player positions), and another to all players in the league, searchable via temporal (last week, last month, this season, previous seasons, month by month each previous season) and generic categories including positions (all running backs, tight ends, linebackers), ownership status (players in my team or that of my immediate opponent, all owned players, all free agents) and rankings (preseason and current). This news and information, as well as changes to the (fantasy) status of players, are all updated constantly, and so the opportunities to pull off a coup are not just confined to daytime hours: fantasy players who are willing to get up in the middle of the night can often be the first to gain access to much sought after free agents, thus improving their squads and gaining an advantage over rivals.

This carries over to practices and sites of television sports spectatorship: when managers watch an NFL game between Detroit and Dallas, for instance, they may be torn between wanting Detroit (whom they support) to win, while hoping that the Dallas running back on their fantasy team scores a couple of touchdowns. At this moment a gap is established up here between two largely antithetical ways of seeing, as Michael Silver, a Yahoo Sport columnist, identifies after an interview he conducted with the St Louis Rams quarterback Marc Bulger:

> Bulger . . . talked about the way fantasy football has changed fans' perspective, reasoning that if he lost a game while putting up big numbers, 'I guess if you throw for a lot of yards, to some people, it's not that bad of a loss.' To real competitors like Bulger, that's beyond annoying, and Sunday had a whole lot of that: Bulger (368 passing yards), the Bengals' Carson Palmer (401 passing yards, six touchdowns) and Johnson (11 catches, 209 yards, two TDs) and the Panthers' Smith (eight catches, 153 yards, three TDs) shined in defeat. I know all of these players well enough to be confident that they're all furious right now, even as their fantasy 'owners' rejoice. (Silver 2007)

Bulger may be watching the same games as fantasy players, but the way he understands, narrates and evaluates them, the criteria he uses, and what he considers correct and proper spectatorship, are of a completely different order to what is practised in fantasy sport. His way of seeing is predicated on a conventional or traditional notion of sports spectatorship, of the kind that characterized American and world sport from the time of college football games in the early part of the twentieth, where fantasy spectators entered into and invested themselves in a fantasy driven relationship with the team, player or even the game itself. Like the ethos that pervades the field of sport, this form of identification is not necessarily dominated by, or reducible to, winning and losing. Some fans are attracted to a club precisely because it has a history of being uncompetitive, or because something about its history has been transformed into cultural capital; the 'curse of the Bambino' doubtlessly worked this way for the Boston Red Sox, whose legions of fans were, for a time, in the curious position of having to come to terms with the fact that they were currently more successful than the rich and powerful and much hated New York Yankees.

Fantasy sport, on the other hand, is more or less incongruent with regard to the field of sport, and its values, logics and imperatives – media and business inflected, or otherwise. As Silver and Bulger make clear, there is no necessary articulation between the performance of a team or player in a real sporting contest and fantasy. In fact the opposite can sometimes be true: if an NFL team is losing badly or even hopelessly, for instance, then its quarterback becomes potentially very valuable because he will have to pass the ball on just about every occasion – and in the process inflate his figures on those of his wide receivers. The gaudy statistics produced by the players referred to in the Silver article testify to this; however, there are far more egregious examples, where players who have performed so poorly that they are in danger of losing their place in real sport play a positive and sometimes decisive role in fantasy contests. This disjunction is even more pronounced in those NFL fantasy leagues that attach a positive value to conventionally negative statistics, and where fumbles, dropped catches, incomplete passes and conceding points are celebrated like touchdowns.

People who take part in fantasy leagues are usually required to be highly knowledgeable, literate and enthusiastic sports fans, connoisseurs rather than laymen, who literally takes sport out of its world or field, and relocate it (players, teams, scores, activities) in an order and community of the literate. Shipman quotes Adam Slotnick of Fox Sports to the effect that fantasy sport 'is tremendously enjoyable and keeps many of us in touch to a greater extent than if the league never existed . . . the fantasy sports world is a world that bonds individuals together into groups with similar likes and dislikes . . . a family if you will' (2005: 34). And he makes the point that:

> Because of the length of a fantasy game – one sports season, so about six months – there is plenty of time for players who do not know one another prior to the season to interact and form lasting relationships. Since many leagues exist year after year with approximately the same set of players, these leagues can generate rivalries between players competing for the league championship as well as more sympathetic relationships between players near the bottom of their leagues. (4)

However, the relatively exclusive status of fantasy sport is changing. Much like the rest of the field of sport, the growth in popularity of and participation in fantasy leagues has meant that:

> media companies recognize fantasy sports as potentially profitable, and . . . one popular fantasy oriented Web site, Sandbox.com, enjoyed revenues of nearly $7 million in 200 after grossing just $200,000 two years earlier. Other similar Web sites have been sold to investors for as much as $20 million. CBS owned SportsLine.com increased its profit by more than one third from 2002 to 2003 thanks to fantasy sports . . . Overall, online media bring in an estimated $500 million annually because of fantasy sports . . . Corporate America has taken notice, too. Callaway Golf Company . . . launched a Fantasy Golf Challenge in . . . 2005 asking participants to . . . select golfers they believe will win predetermined matchups. The top performers each week receive prizes such as golf balls, custom made clubs, or golf vacations. (Woodward 2004: 11)

This incipient split in fantasy sport is manifested and played out on the Australian Rules fantasy website 'FanFooty', which provides updated generic fantasy scores (based on the scoring regimes used by most popular competitions), but divides its screen space more or less evenly between statistical information (updates of scores, goal scorers, injuries, number of possessions, free kicks) on one side and fan comments on the other. The site is useful for experienced and literate fantasy players from small, established leagues because it provides continuously updated (every 30 seconds, approximately 2 minutes behind real time) detailed match statistics that can be translated into any scoring format, no matter how esoteric. These fantasy players are probably present as visitors – simply because there is no other comparable service available for fantasy AFL. They are present as absences, however, from the accompanying 'Fan comments' section, which is almost entirely made up of neophytes playing the bigger, more recent, and simplified mainstream fantasy leagues.

Generally speaking, fantasy sport players tend to watch more sport than other fans (Woodward 2004: 13), so most participants will be relatively literate with regard to the sport on which fantasy league is based. With fantasy competitions, however, neophytes will make strategic decisions that are naïve or even illiterate, such as presuming that ability and cultural capital necessarily translates from, and is comparable across, real and fantasy sport domains. In their study of strategic decision making in online fantasy basketball games Brian Smith, Priya Sharma and Paula Hooper concluded 'It was also apparent that domain specific knowledge use differed between novice and expert players' (Smith et al. 2006: 354). One obvious point of differentiation was what they referred to as the 'recognition heuristic', which in fantasy sport 'translates into choosing athletes by virtue of name recognition' (354). They found that inexperienced fantasy players were more likely:

> to create their teams using the recognition heuristic. Experienced players are able to use additional knowledge to choose athletes. Indeed, some players explicitly stated that they did not rely on name athletes when building their teams . . . Some players simply choose athletes from their favorite NBA teams without considering their statistical performances. For instance, Houston Rockets fans might always select players from that team out of sheer devotion rather than looking closely at statistics to find athletes who might accrue higher points totals . . . Such decisions are primarily based on loyalty to a city/team . . . Recognition and team loyalty strategies are most likely to be used by novices. (354)

The other form of strategic illiteracy found in the actions and discourses of novice players, frequently manifested on the 'FanFooty' discussion facility, is a lack of consideration of time and context. The participants who drop and add, praise and dismiss, and trade and acquire players 'on the spur of the moment', so to speak, are taken in by statistical aberrations and display a lack of understanding of context: a player may appear to be performing poorly in a game, but that performance may need to be re-evaluated if, for instance, it happened while playing against a good defensive team that consistently limited opponents scores.

Conclusion

There is a strong continuity between fantasy sport and interactive media sport, but there are also several crucial differences. First, while they are both informed by the same basic characteristics (bringing the audience into the activity, a hystericizing of spectatorship), in fantasy sport they operate in a manner that is more accentuated, pervasive and intense. Interactive websites and television allow audiences to become part of the spectacle/event (as commentators and analysts, articulating the voice of the fan group), and to make personalized decisions about how and what they will watch (game choices, multiscreen options, camera angles, zoom functions). Fantasy sites and games not only move audiences/participants into the activity of real sport: to a large extent the game/sporting league, its players and their statistics function as the material on which the fantasy competition is based. In other words, while the principle of interactivity generally produces audience activity as complementary with regard to sport, with fantasy sport the original event is largely taken over by the fantasy league and its logics, and becomes a virtual simulation of itself.

The same distinction applies to the issues of spectatorship and visual regimes. Although interactive television disposes spectatorial vision to look intensely, all the time, from every angle, at as many incidents and activities in as many games as possible (theoretically in an attempt to increase the productivity of vision and to identify more detail and significance), in the end there is still a (visual) identification that binds the audience to the field of sport and its events. The self that is located in the field of vision remains within the traditional role of the fan watching sport – even if the picture is now enlarged to include not just the event as visual object, but also the fan watching (and to some extent, contributing to or even making) sport. There is certainly some kind of visual enhancement at work here. Technology not only disposes and facilitates continuous mobile vision, it also foregrounds watching as an active and productive process: the game that I watch is marked with and produced out of my work, my choices, my literacies. But I watch and enhance that sporting event largely within its own parameters and logics. This is not the case with fantasy sport: when I watch an NFL game as a fantasy sport manager the issue of what is significant or not is displaced from any conventional NFL regime or context. A small gain made by a running back, for instance, may be completely inconsequential as far as the state of the actual game is concerned, but it can be of vital importance to thousands of fantasy leagues. Moreover, the identity of that running back is extracted from the NFL team and taken to and spread, at a virtual level, just as widely. His affiliation with Detroit or Dallas is not irrelevant, but it is now largely intertextual: it functions, not with regard to itself, but as a trace (this is where he came out of when drafted him) and a context (the team emphasizes the passing game, so this running back will have limited value in fantasy leagues).

The most crucial difference between the two areas, however, is tied up with the functional relationship new media interactivity and the distinction Pierre Bourdieu makes between sporting audiences as 'connoisseurs' and/or 'laymen'. Bourdieu suggests that the media's attempts to widen audiences for media sport means taking the sporting event 'to a public very imperfectly equipped with the specific competence needed to decipher it adequately' (1991: 364). Media interactivity, in this context, has a number of important functions, all of which are designed to keep that wider audience attentive and interested, specifically in the face of sport's 'violence and confusion'. As well as the obvious advantage of providing pedagogical tools and advice (visual and scriptural), interactivity provides the laymen with both the illusion of literacy via participation, and the ability to navigate away from the chaotic in order to settle on and enjoy what is known, understood and appreciated by the layman. Literacy as participation takes the form of the website inviting you in, as a participant and equal, 'one of us', and a member of the field (fan, analyst, spectator, enthusiast). The fact that the general viewers' comments and contributions to the BBC Sport website are completely inane and superficial only helps to naturalize that sense of belonging, since there is nothing (no performance of acuity, no opportunity for the highly literate to articulate literacy) to mark out or distinguish one contribution ('Great goal') from another ('We need to hang on'). Similarly with interactive television, what is offered, and is of particular value, to the neophyte is the performance and illusion of control – I may not understand particularly well what is happening, but I can make the game up to suit myself. This interactive facility also caters to the inattentive viewer: if 'nothing is happening', they can switch from one game to another, split and resplit screens, or follow specific players until something appears or happens that appeals to them.

Fantasy sport constitutes a form of play as escape from what many connoisseurs of sport doubtlessly consider sport has become; that is, a commercialized, trivialized and hyperbolized media spectacle. However, this form of escape is increasingly being played out in and through the technologies and spaces of the media-as-business: consequently, fantasy sport is becoming mainstream, with large public and simplified public leagues, fantasy sport conventions and a Hall of Fame (Zillgitt 2000). In order to increase participation, one click fantasy games are being developed 'that call for one or two minutes a day as opposed to the research needed to stay up on day by day fantasy leagues' (Passan 2008); and a legal battle is taking place between fantasy sport providers and sport leagues over the requirement that the former pay fees in order to use statistics (Passan 2008). All this points to 'the transmogrification' of fantasy sport 'into just another business' (Passan 2008), aimed increasingly at the layman rather than the connoisseur.

CHAPTER TEN

Conclusion

In 2012 Channel Nine, which has exclusive rights to the broadcasting of cricket in Australia, produced a series of television commercials for the upcoming season which featured a tour by Sri Lanka with test, one-day and twenty–twenty games. The tone across the advertisements differed to some extent, depending on the form of the game being featured (there was more of a sense of gravitas with the tests, for instance) but the discourses that were utilized were quite similar. Instead of concentrating on shots of cricketing action involving recognizable star players (Michael Clark, Lasith Malinga), the visuals tended to feature the crowd: they were shown wearing costumes (superheroes, nurses, cartoon characters); providing entertainment (playing musical instruments, singing); and dancing, gesticulating and celebrating. Prizes were offered for the best costumes, the games were referred to as 'day outs', and the tenor and genre was clearly that of an exuberant fancy dress party. In one of the commercials the setting actually is a party: the camera follows as a crowd filters into and wanders through a large house eating, drinking and dancing to a band, until it reaches a room where there is a green strip of artificial turf; two batsmen run through the crowd onto the pitch, where they warm up in time with the music.

These commercials are advertising sporting contests – while making minimal or perfunctory references to sport. This approach is becoming more common in sports advertising. It is expected of an event such as the Wellington Rugby Sevens, where the media coverage and interviews are almost exclusively focused on the costumes and the partying; or the World Darts Championship, which relies on and plays up to its noisy and interactive indoor crowds. However, the focus on the game as a site of carnival and partying in more mainstream and high profile sports (cricket, football, rugby, cycling) is a recent development. We made the point in our first chapter that discourses make the objects that they supposedly describe, and that the discursive trajectory and genealogy of the field of sport enables us to trace any changes and transformations that have taken place within it and in terms of its relation to the wider social field – in terms of how it understands and articulates itself, its values, and the kinds of socio-cultural work it performs. From this perspective the Channel Nine cricketing commercials, and similar advertisements and other media texts that emphasize the entertainment value of Premier League, IPL, Olympic and Tour de France crowds and spectators, are discursive statements that constitute and manifest a significant shift in the contemporary cultural field of sport. They don't just produce sporting contests as affective-driven entertainments: more importantly they also position sport as being subordinated to and dependant upon the patronage of demographics which have little or no investment in the thing itself; and by extension they relegate the habitus, ethos and imperatives of traditional sport to the status of a series of low key marketing slogans.

The modern field of sport started out as an extension of public school athletics; gradually morphed into a popular and commercial – and eventually, global – cultural activity that served as an important site for communal identity and identification; and then was incorporated into the logics and discourses of the capitalist media spectacle.

However, discursive changes within the field have generally been reasonably slow and accretive: variations with regard to the values, rules, practices and ethos associated with the sporting habitus have tended to develop with what Appadurai refers to as 'glacial force' (1996: 6); and even when the habitus has undergone change, displaced values and dispositions have usually retained much of their original capital. The institutions and forces that transformed folk football into public school athletics, for example, carefully and strategically integrated the concept and sensibility of play into the discourses and bodily hexis of what was in effect a disciplinary and pedagogical regime. The role of athletics in instilling and naturalizing an upper-class sense of superiority and distinction is dependant on subjects maintaining and performing, at all times but most particularly in moments of utmost intensity, duress and commitment, a disinterested relation to the thing. This disinterestedness is understood and approached as a matter of form: what distinguishes the elite amateur from the lower-class professional, or even from the amateur worker taking part in a game of football in the local competition, is that the latter will try too hard, and show that they are trying; in other words winning or losing means more to them than their commitment to and identification with the game as ethos.

The disinterestedness of public school athletics mimics the sensibility and generic characteristics of play, in that the utility of athletics (learning to be part of a team, developing resilience and an ability to think under pressure) is not emphasized or a point of focus. While nineteenth-century headmasters might praise and celebrate sport for its ability to create gentlemen and leaders, this process was not understood as being commensurate with a shaping of raw material or a learning exercise; if this was the case, then the sons (and presumably daughters) of the working class might just as well play and benefit from sport. The main point of athletics, emphasized strongly in a work such as *Tom Brown's Schooldays*, was that it helped gentlemen to discover qualities and virtues that they already possessed, at least potentially, by virtue of being gentlemen. This is why an adherence to the form of play as a voluntary and wasteful activity was both necessary and well suited to the discursive regime of athletics. The students of Eton, Harrow and Winchester could not be seen to be working on the football and cricket fields in order to make something out of themselves: they were simply wasting their time and enjoying themselves, which ensured that they walked away as the gentlemen they already were.

A similar discursive continuity can be seen in the transition from public school athletics to popular, spectator-driven sport as it emerged in Britain towards the end of the nineteenth century. Although amateurs were gradually superseded by professionals in major sports such as cricket and football, institutions and governing bodies were dominated by upper- and middle-class officials from public school backgrounds. This meant that cricket in England, for instance, did not undergo much change until the late twentieth century: the finances of the county game remained disorganized and haphazard; the attitude of the MCC and the County Clubs to the media was unenthusiastic, uncooperative and suspicious; and the commitment to and maintenance of the amateur–professional division meant that when Len Hutton was appointed in the 1950s, he became the first professional captain of England or the MCC since the second half of the nineteenth century. Football authorities were almost as conservative as their cricketing counterparts: they remained isolationist and disdainful with regard to international competitions (Goldblatt 2007: 239), and openly hostile towards or suspicious of women's football, floodlit games, radio coverage of games, players' rights, pools competitions and technological innovations. By the late nineteenth century the FA had 'made its peace, albeit with regret, with the forces of commercialism and professionalism, but no further shift in that direction would be tolerated' (184).

In the first half of the twentieth century, sport underwent significant changes, largely as a consequence of the field becoming increasingly globalized. In the United States major sports such as baseball, boxing and college football were integrated into an incipient media–sports nexus; professional football leagues and strong spectator cultures developed in Central Europe and South America; and in the British Empire cricket took on some of the cultural inflections and values of the various host countries – in Australia, for instance, the prestigious position of test team captain was occupied by a player who had to be worth his place in the side, rather than being reserved for a symbolic amateur presence. There were countermovements, such as the modern Olympic games, which rearticulated the ethos of public school athletics within a more modern and internationalist framework; but the discursive purity of Coubertin's vision was from the beginning forced to resist, accommodate, deal with or simply pretend not to notice political interventions and conflicts, professionalism, partisan spectators, the media and the female athletes.

We have argued that the transformation of the cultural field of sport from elitist, public school and Victorian athletics into a popular, spectator-driven, professional and heavily mediatized set of activities, events and discourses involved a complete change in its socio-cultural functions. Whereas sport initially had a pedagogical and normative function producing gentlemen and leaders, from the 1890s onward it increasingly interpellated subjects-as-communities – as members of towns, cities, religious groups, class factions, ethnicities and nations. The discourses of sport developed and expanded accordingly: while notions of self-overcoming, competition, play, sporting behaviour and team work remained relatively sacrosanct, they were now joined by an ethics of identification and commitment involving both the players and spectators and fans. Sport became an occasion for the playing out of and enjoyment that derived from the 'between us' of communal identity; and to participate in sport in a casual or non-professional local competition constituted an extension of that this process of identification, at both a specific (the local team and players) and general (the culture, form and discourse of sport) sense. In this guise, sport attracted and was played and watched by a wide and ever increasing range of demographics; this meant that it increasingly drew the interest of the media, and by extension that various aspects and sites of sport, from participation to spectatorship, were brought into what Appadurai (1988) calls the commodity phase or situation.

The tension between the more autonomous and traditional values and institutions of sport, and the imperatives associated with the media and commercialization, was manifested at a discursive level throughout the twentieth century, although in different ways across the temporal and spatial continuum of the field. In some sports there was a relative homogeneity across quite diverse national sporting cultures; so cricket and rugby, for instance, remained committed to traditional discourses, values and practices until the Packer intervention in cricket in the 1970s and the introduction of professionalism in rugby in the 1990s. The Olympic movement continued to maintain a strong discursive and practical connection to its founding ethos until its incorporation into Cold War politics and the media spectacle in the 1970s and 1980s. Rugby league's largely working-class culture was swept away, simultaneously in both the north of England and the east coast of Australia, when the game was effectively taken over by Rupert Murdoch's News Limited in the 1990s.

As Bourdieu has explained (1991) this intense mediatization and commoditization of sport has effectively changed the discourses and culture of the field, and the kind of cultural work that it undertakes and performs.

The Football World Cup, for instance, is now predominantly played out by and for:

> the media and for consortia locked into headlong competition. Among the social effects of this 'mediatisation' of football are to be found: the increase in the number of matches (with the growth of European and international competitions); the increase in the number of matches televised; the trend for pay-TV channels to obtain exclusive rights for matches; the fact that the time and date of matches are more and more determined by the needs of television; changes to the structure of competitions; corruption scandals; the birth of globe-trotting cosmopolitan players, often . . . changing clubs every two or three years . . . the effect of which is to transform the relationship between supporters and players. (Bourdieu et al. 1998: 18)

The relationship between supporters and teams has also been transformed by the media and commercialization: identification with a sport, team or player has itself been commoditized in a variety of ways, involving everything from selling seats, memberships or broadcast subscriptions to promoting tourist-oriented trips that combine attendance at the games and privileged access to the players with tours to places of scenic beauty or historical interest. Commoditization now discursively inhabits virtually every minute of every television or internet broadcast: as a game is progressing, viewers are invited to text in and predict the final score, who will be player of the match, to bet on various outcomes, and to make comments about controversial decisions; and the commentary on the current game is often the departure point for advertising and promoting the next televised match.

Sport has moved into that phase of late capitalism where, according to Baudrillard (2003), emphasis has shifted from the relation between the production and consumption of goods and services to the production of desires; for instance, more or less every week of the season Channel Nine in Australia takes advantage of any event or milestone that brings a cricketer media attention (an outstanding century, retirement, five thousand test runs) to offer 'collector's items' that commemorate the occasion or event, such as a limited edition of signed bats or photographs. The idea is to produce a desire for something that is a more or less limitless nothing, since just about anything can be arbitrarily designated as desirable and a form of capital. What is put in play here is an imperative to desire a desire; and from this production of a desire the spectator is disposed to consume, to be involved, to get closer or live out the fantasy of a privileged attachment to the sport, match, event, team or player.

The logical extension of this process is for the spectators and fans to become the thing itself; that is, for the 'between us' that discursively joins supporters and teams to be transformed into a process whereby the supporter symbolically alienates and incorporates a sport through commodity consumption. In fantasy and interactive media sport, for instance, the traditional relationship between the physical activity of sport and the ethos towards which it is discursively oriented (self-overcoming, helping the team win, representing the community) is largely replaced by a different set of logics and orientations. With media interactivity the sites of sport function predominantly to allow fans to appear within, and become part of, the mediatized game-as-spectacle. This imperative carries over and animates the 'spectator culture' that we referred to at the beginning of this chapter: the scoring of a goal or a player being sent off now offers an opportunity for spectators to perform for the cameras by celebrating or protesting in a particularly idiosyncratic or spectacular fashion. Much like players on the field, the sporting crowd is constantly playing to and for the cameras: they draw attention to themselves by dancing, being passionate and emotional, holding up signs, or through wearing unusual, colourful or skimpy costumes. Sporting events have become 'affect factories': the enjoyment, passion and performances of the crowd are taken up and used to commoditize the game for a wider demographic of media spectators around the world.

This does not mean that earlier discourses or values have been disappeared, or no longer carry out any socio-cultural function or work – either within or outside the field. The role that sport has taken on as a site for the interpellation of communal identity, along the cultural capital that has accrued to that work, means that some areas of women's sport have become relatively legitimized and professionalized, and now receive considerably more media attention. Given that for over 150 years sport-as-discourse has had a history of partaking in and providing justification for symbolic violence directed towards women, the increasing legitimation of women's sport constitutes a positive development in gender politics. Moreover, discourses of sport as a privileged cultural space characterized by fairness and justice continue to be reproduced, deployed and celebrated in popular culture. In Ken Loach's *Looking for Eric* the figure of Eric Cantona stands in for and embodies an ethical relation to life and community that is taken straight from traditional and, despite the lower-class context, even foundational discourses of sport; and in films such as *Field of Dreams*, *Remember the Titans* and *Bend It Like Beckham* sport is conceived of as a form of socio-cultural value-as-magic that has the potential to transform and redeem people, communities and wider society.

This ambiguous status of the traditional discourses of sport in the twentieth century is perhaps best characterized by Slavoj Zizek's notion of a discourse that is 'between two deaths' (1992: 131). The two deaths exist at the level of the real and the symbolic: a discourse can be superseded, rendered anachronistic or exist only as an empty performative (the Olympic oath, or two football teams shaking hands before playing a bitterly contested local derby, are examples of this), but until its real death can be known and formally articulated, it remains symbolically alive – or at least unburied. As Zizek writes, this is the logic of a dream reported in Freud's *Interpretation of Dreams* regarding a father 'who does not know that he is dead: the point is . . . that because he does not know that he is dead, he continues to live – he must be reminded of his death . . . he is still living because he has forgotten to die' (134).

The integration of the field of sport into the media spectacle provides a very good reason why the body of sport's foundational and traditional discourses has not been given up for burial: it still constitutes the mechanism that motivates a subject's passionate identification with and attachment to the thing as a potential commodity; in other words, traditional sports discourses are too valuable to be allowed to die. Staying with a Freudian motif, we can refer to his account in *Totem and Taboo* (1985) of the process whereby the father of the primal human horde, having been murdered by his disaffected sons, remains a discursive and symbolic presence, even 'stronger than the living one had been' (204). The process whereby an aura is associated with the figure of the dead father, Freud argues, is the result of a 'filial sense of guilt' (205); the sons, realizing the enormity of their crime, set up a network of taboos, rules, laws and prohibitions in the name of the father that are also sacred to the father, and anyone openly violating them has to be punished because their act is a reminder of the original act of violence upon which the fraternal community was founded.

We need to develop and complicate this narrative if we are going to apply it to sport in the late twentieth century and beyond; a sense of guilt does not animate or direct the logics, interests and forces that maintain, deploy and articulate, with almost a religious conviction and intensity, the ethos of sport. And yet there are events where a relation to that ethos is performed and reaffirmed, almost in spite of and certainly contrary to dominant commercial discourses and values. Think of the discursive and symbolic violence directed towards sporting figures who have been exposed as cheats, from baseball's Shoeless Joe Jackson (who infamously helped throw a World Series) to cycling's Lance Armstrong; and what this says about the field and its relation to sport as ethos and value. Jackson has taken on an iconic status in American sport as the figure who manifested a truth that America would rather not know. In the film *Field of Dreams* his ghost returns to repurify and animate the spirit of baseball; he comes back to play for the pure enjoyment of playing, thus renouncing everything that destroyed his reputation and the game he played – money, betting and cheating. The logic is much the same with Armstrong: by admitting his guilt in organizing the doping regime that enabled him to win seven consecutive Tours de France, he was doing nothing more than making public a knowledge that was understood and accepted by anyone with the slightest familiarity with professional cycling. However, by admitting that cycling (and by extension, modern sport) necessarily involves and even requires cheating, Armstrong makes it harder for sports fans and the media to believe what they need to believe (that sport is about pure competition, self-overcoming and the imperative to play) if they are to commit to, accept, exchange, experience, identify with and enjoy the stories and moments of sporting achievements, heroics and triumphs.

BIBLIOGRAPHY

Adams, J. (2006), 'Pater's Muscular Aestheticism', in D. Hall (ed.), *Muscular Christianity*. Cambridge: Cambridge University Press.
Adelman, M. (1986), *A Sporting Time*. Urbana: University of Illinois Press.
— (1997), 'The Early Years of Baseball, 1845–60', in S. Pope (ed.), *The New American Sport History*. Urbana: University of Illinois Press.
Aitchison, C. (ed.) (2007), *Sport and Gendered Identities*. London: Routledge.
Allen, D. (2006), 'Young England: Muscular Christianity and the Politics of the Body in Tom Brown's Schooldays', in D. Hall (ed.), *Muscular Christianity*. Cambridge: Cambridge University Press.
Anderson, B. (1991), *Imagined Communities*. London: Verso.
Andrews, D. (2004), 'Sport in the Late Capitalist Moment', in T. Slack (ed.), *The Commercialization of Sport*. London: Routledge.
— (2009), 'Sport, Culture and Late Capitalism', in B. Carrington and I. McDonald (eds), *Marxism, Cultural Studies and Sport*. London: Routledge.
Andrews, D. and Jackson, S. (2001), 'Introduction: Sports Celebrities, Public Culture, and Private Experience', in D. Andrews and S. Jackson (eds), *Sports Stars*. London: Routledge.
Appadurai, A. (1988), 'Introduction: Commodities and the Politics of Value', in A. Appadurai (ed.), *The Social Life of Things*. Cambridge: Cambridge University Press.
— (1997), *Modernity at Large*. Minneapolis: Minnesota University Press.
Arnold, M. (1979), *Culture and Anarchy*. Cambridge: Cambridge University Press.
Austin, J. L. (1975), *How to Do Things with Words*. Oxford: Clarendon.
Baker, W. (1982), *Sports in the Western World*. Totowa, NJ: Rowman and Littlefield.
Bakhtin, M. (1984), *Rabelais and His World*. Bloomington: Indiana University Press.
Bale, J. (2001), *Sport, Space and the City*. Caldwell: Blackburn.
Bale, J. and Christensen, M. (2004a), 'Introduction: Post-Olympism', in J. Bale and M. Christensen (eds), *Post-Olympism?* Oxford: Berg.
— (eds) (2004b), *Post-Olympism?* Oxford: Berg.
Barthes, R. (1979), *Image-Music-Text*, trans. S. Heath. Glasgow: Fontana.
Bataille, G. (1989), *Visions of Excess*. Minneapolis: University of Minnesota Press.
— (1991), *The Accursed Share: Volumes 11 and 111*. New York: Zone Books.
Baudrillard, J. (2003), *The Consumer Society*. London: Sage.
Belanger, A. (2009), 'Towards a Critical Political Economy of Sport', in B. Carrington and I. McDonald (eds), *Marxism, Cultural Studies and Sport*. London: Routledge.

Bhabha, H. (1994), *The Location of Culture*. London: Routledge.

Birch, D., Schirato, T. and Srivastava, S. (2001), *Asia: Cultural Politics in the Global Age*. Sydney: Allen & Unwin.

Birley, D. (1995), *Land of Hope and Glory: Sport and British Society 1887–1910*. Manchester: Manchester University Press.

— (2003), *A Social History of English Cricket*. London: Aurum Press.

Booth, D. (2005), *The Field: Truth and Fiction in Sport History*. London: Routledge.

Bourdieu, P. (1989), *Distinction*. London: Routledge.

— (1991), 'Sport and Social Class', in C. Mukerji and M. Schudson (eds), *Rethinking Popular Culture*. Berkeley: University of California Press.

— (1993), *The Field of Cultural Production*. Cambridge: Polity.

— (1995), *The Rules of Art*. Stanford: Stanford University Press.

— (1998a), *On Television and Journalism*. London: Pluto Press.

— (1998b), *The State Nobility*. Cambridge: Polity.

— (2000), *Pascalian Meditations*. Cambridge: Polity.

— (2005), *Language and Symbolic Power*, trans. G. Raymond and M. Adamson. Cambridge: Polity.

— (2010), *Sociology Is a Martial Art*, trans. P. Ferguson, R. Nice and L. Wacquant. New York: New Press.

Bourdieu, P. and Wacquant, L. (1992), *An Invitation to Reflexive Sociology*. Cambridge: Polity.

Bourdieu, P., Dauncey, H. and Hare, G. (1998), 'The State, Economics and Sport', *Sport in Society* 1(2), 15–21.

Boyle, R. and Haynes, R. (2000), *Power Play: Sport, the Media and Popular Culture*. Harlow: Pearson.

Brailsford, D. (1991), *Sport, Time and Society*. London: Routledge.

Butler, J. (1990), *Gender Trouble*. New York: Routledge.

— (1993), *Bodies That Matter*. New York: Routledge.

— (1997), *Excitable Speech*. New York: Routledge.

Caillois, R. (2001), *Men, Play and Games*. Urbana: University of Illinois Press.

Carpentier, F. and Lefevre, J.-P. (2008), ' The Modern Olympic Movement, Women's Sport and the Social Order during the Inter-War Period', in B. Majumdar and S. Collins (eds), *Olympism: The Global Vision*. London: Routledge.

Carrington, B. (2009), 'Cultural Studies/Marxism/Sport', in B. Carrington and I. McDonald (eds), *Marxism, Cultural Studies and Sport*. London: Routledge.

Carrington, B. and McDonald, I. (eds) (2001), *Race, Sport and British Society*. London: Routledge.

— (eds) (2009), *Marxism, Cultural Studies and Sport*. London: Routledge.

Cashmore, E. (1990), *Making Sense of Sport*. London: Routledge.

— (2000), *Sports Culture: An A–Z Guide*. London: Routledge.

Certeau, M. de (1988), *The Practice of Everyday Life*. Berkeley: University of California Press.

Coubertin, P. de (2000), *Olympism*. Lausanne: International Olympic Committee.

Crary, J. (1998), *Techniques of the Observer*. Cambridge: MIT Press.

Crawford, G. (2004), *Fans, Sport and Culture*. London: Routledge.

Cronin, M. (1999), *Sport and Nationalism in Ireland*. Dublin: Four Courts.

Debord, G. (2006), *The Society of the Spectacle*, trans. D. Nicholson-Smith. New York: Zone Books.

Dunning, E. (2007), 'Sport, Gender and Civilization', in A. Tomlinson (ed.), *The Sports Studies Reader*. London: Routledge.

Eichberg, H. (2004), 'The Global, the Popular and the Inter-Popular', in J. Bale and M. Christensen (eds), *Post-Olympism?* Oxford: Berg.

Elias, N. (2000), *The Civilizing Process*. Oxford: Blackwell.

Elias, N. and Dunning, E. (1993), *Quest for Excitement*. Oxford: Blackwell.

Fest, J. (1977), *Hitler*. Harmondsworth: Penguin.

Foucault, M. (1972), *The Archaeology of Knowledge*. New York: Pantheon.

— (1973), *The Order of Things*. New York: Vintage.

— (1986a), *Language, Counter-Memory, Practice*, trans. D. Bouchard and S. Simon. New York: Cornell University Press.

— (1986b), *The Use of Pleasure*, trans. R. Hurley. New York: Vintage.

— (1988), *The Care of the Self*, trans. R. Hurley. New York: Vintage.

— (1997), *Ethics: The Essential Works Volume 1*, trans. R. Hurley et al. London: Allen Lane.

— (1998), *Aesthetics, Methodology and Epistemology: Essential Works of Foucault 1954–84 Volume 2*, trans. R. Hurley et al. New York: New Press.

— (2001), *Power: The Essential Works Volume 3*, trans. R. Hurley et al. London: Allen Lane.

— (2003), *Society Must Be Defended*, trans. D. Macey. London: Allen Lane.

— (2005), *The Hermeneutics of the Subject*, trans. G. Burchell. New York: Picador.

— (2007), *Security, Territory, Population*, trans. G. Burchell. New York: Palgrave Macmillan.

— (2008a), *The Birth of Biopolitics*, trans. G. Burchell. London: Palgrave Macmillan.

— (2008b), *The History of Sexuality Volume 1*. London: Penguin.

— (2010), *The Government of Self and Others*, trans. G. Burchell. London: Palgrave Macmillan.

— (2011), *The Courage of Truth*, trans. G. Burchell. London: Palgrave Macmillan.

Freud, S. (1985), *The Origins of Religion*, trans. J. Strachey. Harmondsworth: Penguin.

Frow, J. (1997), *Time and Commodity Culture*. Oxford: Clarendon Press.

— (2006), *Genre*. London Routledge.

Girard, R. (1988), *To Double Business Bound*. Baltimore: Johns Hopkins University Press.

Goff, B. (2011), 'Introduction', in B. Goff and M. Simpson (eds), *Thinking the Olympics*. London: Bristol Classics Press.

Goff, B. and Simpson, M. (eds) (2011), *Thinking the Olympics*. London: Bristol Classics Press.

Goldblatt, D. (2007), *The Ball Is Round: A Global History of Football*. London: Penguin.

Gorn, E. (1997), 'Sports through the Nineteenth Century', in A. Pope (ed.), *The New American Sport History*. Urbana: University of Illinois Press.

Guha, R. (2003), *Corner of a Foreign Field*. London: Picador.

Guttmann, A. (1978), *From Ritual to Record*. New York: Columbia University Press.

— (1986), *Sports Spectators*. New York: Columbia University Press.

— (1991), *Women's Sport*. New York: Columbia University Press.

— (1992), *The Olympics, a History of the Modern Games*. Urbana: University of Illinois Press.

— (1994), *Games and Empire*. New York: Columbia University Press.

— (1995), 'Puritans at Play? Accusations and Replies', in D. Wiggins (ed.), *Sport in America*. Champaign, IL: Human Kinetics.

— (1996), *The Erotic in Sport*. New York: Columbia University Press.

Hall, D. (ed.) (2006), *Muscular Christianity*. Cambridge: Cambridge University Press.

Hargreaves, Jennifer (1994), *Sporting Females*. London: Routledge.

Hargreaves, John (1987), *Sport, Power and Culture*. Cambridge: Polity.

Hay, R. (2003), 'The Last Night of the Poms: Australia as a Postcolonial Sporting society?' in J. Bale and M. Cronin (eds), *Sport and Postcolonialism*. Oxford: Berg.

Hill, J. (2002), *Sport, Leisure & Culture in Twentieth Century Britain*. New York: Palgrave.

Holt, R. (1989), *Sport and the British*. Oxford: Clarendon Press.

Holt, R. and Mason, T. (2000), *Sport in Britain 1945–2000*. Oxford: Blackwell.

Horne, J. (2006), *Sport in Consumer Culture*. New York: Palgrave.

Houlihan, B. (2004), 'Sports Globalisation, the State and the Problem of Governance', in T. Slack (ed.), *The Commercialization of Sport*. London: Routledge.

Hughes, T. (1974), *Tom Brown's Schooldays*. London: Macmillan.

Hughson, J. (2009), *The Making of Sporting Cultures*. London: Routledge.

Huizinga, J. (1966), *Homo Ludens*. Boston: Beacon Press.

Hutchins, B. (2005), 'Unity, Difference and the National Game: Cricket and Australian National Identity', in S. Wagg (ed.), *Cricket and National Identity in the Postcolonial Age*. London: Routledge.

Isidore, C. (2003), 'The Ultimate Fantasy – Profits', CNNMoney.com money.cnn. com/2003/08/29/commentary/column_sportsbiz/sportsbiz/index.htm

Jackson, S., Grainger, A. and Batty, R. (2004), 'Media Sport, Globalization and the Challenge to Commercialism', in T. Slack (ed.), *The Commercialization of Sport*. London: Routledge.

James, C. (1963), *Beyond a Boundary*. London: Hutchinson.

Jenkyns, R. (1980), *Victorians and Ancient Greece*. Oxford: Blackwell.

Johnson, R. (1995), 'Editor's Introduction', in P. Bourdieu (ed.), *The Field of Cultural Production*. Cambridge: Polity Press.

Keys, B. (2006), *Globalizing Sport*. Cambridge: Harvard University Press.

Kruger, A. (2004), 'What's the Difference between Propaganda for Tourism or for a Political Regime', in J. Bale and M. Christensen (ed.), *Post-Olympism*. Oxford: Berg.

Lefort, C. (1986), *The Political Forms of Modern Society*. Cambridge: MIT Press.

Lenskyj, H. (2004), 'Making the World Safe for Global Capitalism', in J. Bale and M. Christensen (eds), *Post-Olympism?* Oxford: Berg.

McDevitt, P. (2004), *May the Best Man Win*. New York: Palgrave.

McDonald, I. (2009), 'Revolutionary Marxism and the Critiques of Sport', in B. Carrington and I. McDonald (eds), *Marxism, Cultural Studies and Sport*. London: Routledge.

McIntosh, P. (1987), *Sport in Society*. London: West London Press.

McLuhan, M. (1997), *Essential McLuhan*. London: Routledge.

Magdalinski, T. and Nauright, J. (2004), 'Commercialization of the Modern Olympics', in T. Slack (ed.), *The Commercialization of Sport*. London: Routledge.

Majumdar, B. and Collins, S. (eds) (2008), *Olympism: The Global Vision*. London: Routledge.

Mandell, R. (1984), *Sport in History*. New York: Columbia University Press.

Mangan, J. (1981), *Athleticism in the Victorian and Edwardian Public School*. Cambridge: Cambridge University Press.

— (1999), 'Prologue', in J. Mangan (ed.), *Sport in Europe*. London: Frank Cass.

— (ed.) (2002), *Reformers, Sport, Modernizers*. London: Frank Cass.

Mason, T. (1980), *Association Football and English Society: 1865–1915*. Brighton: Harvester.

Mattelart, A. (1994), *Mapping World Communication*, trans. S. Emanuel and J. Cohen. Minneapolis: University of Minnesota Press.

— (2000), *Networking the World: 1794–2000*, trans. L. Carey-Libbrecht and J. Cohen. Minneapolis: University of Minnesota Press.

— (2003), *The Information Society*, trans. S. Taponier and J. Cohen. London: Sage.

Mauss, M. (1988), *The Gift*. London: Routledge.

Middleton, A. (2007), 'Marking Boundaries', in A. Tomlinson (ed.), *The Sports Studies Reader*. London: Routledge.

Miller, T. (2009), 'Michel Foucault and the Critique of Sport', in B. Carrington and I. McDonald (eds), *Marxism, Cultural Studies and Sport*. London: Routledge.

Miller, T., Lawrence, G., McKay, J. and Rowe, D. (2001), *Globalization and Sport*. London: Sage.

Moeller, V. (2004), 'Doping and the Olympic Games from an Aesthetic Perspective', in J. Bale and M. Christensen (eds), *Post-Olympism?* Oxford: Berg.

Money, T. (1997), *Manly and Muscular Diversions*. London: Duckworth.

Moran, A. (2006), *Understanding the Global TV Format*. Bristol: Intellect Books.

Nietzsche, F. (1956), *The Birth of Tragedy and The Genealogy of Morals*, trans. F. Golffing. New York: Doubleday.

— (1974), *The Gay Science*, trans. W. Kaufmann. New York: Vintage.

Passan, J. (2008), 'The Reality of Fantasy', Yahoo Sports Website http://sports.yahoo.com/mlb/news?slug=jpfantasy042006&prov=yhoo&type=lgns

Peirce, C. (1958), *Selected Writings*. New York: Dover.

Polley, M. (1998), *Moving the Goalposts*. London: Routledge.

— (2007), *Sports History*. New York: Palgrave.

Pope, S. (ed.) (1997), *The New American Sport History*. Urbana: University of Illinois Press.

Riess, S. (1995), *Sport in Industrial America*. Wheeling, IL: Harlan Davidson.

— (1997), 'Sport and the Redefinition of Middle-Class Masculinity in Victorian America', in S. Pope (ed.), *The New American Sport History*. Urbana: University of Illinois Press.

Riordan, J. (1977), *Sport in Soviet Society*. Cambridge: Cambridge University Press.

Roberts, R. and Olson, J. (1997), 'The Roone Revolution', in D. Wiggins (ed.), *Sport in America*. Champaign, IL: Human Kinetics.

Roche, M. (2000), *Mega-Events and Modernity*. London: Routledge.

Sandiford, K. (1994), *Cricket and the Victorians*. Aldershot: Scholar Press.

Sandvoss, C. (2003), *A Game of Two Halves*. London: Routledge.

Schirato, T., Danaher, G. and Webb, J. (2012), *Understanding Foucault*. London: Sage.

Scott, R. (2012), *The Last Expedition*. London: Vintage.

Scrambler, G. (2005), *Sport and Society*. Maidenhead: Open University.

Shipman, F. (2005), 'Blending the Real and Virtual: Activity and Spectatorship in Fantasy Sport', Centre for the Study of Digital Libraries and Department of Computer Science Texas A & M University www.csdl.tamu.edu/~shipman/papers/dac01.pdf

Silk, M. (2004), 'Televised Sport in the Global Consumer Age', in T. Slack (ed.), *The Commercialization of Sport*. London: Routledge.

Silver, M. (2007), 'Morning Rush: Defiant and Dominant', Yahoo Sports Website http://sports.yahoo.com/nfl/news;_ylt=AiYdWCSOw_IxI.HO.j7lhsl5nYcB?slug=msmorningrush091707&prov=yhoo&type=lgns

Slack, T. (ed.) (2004), *The Commercialization of Sport*. London: Routledge.

Smith, B., Sharma, P. and Hooper, P. (2006), 'Decision Making in Online Fantasy Sports Communities', *Interactive Technology and Smart Education* 4, 347–60 www.personal.psu.edu/bks12/papers/ITSE.pdf

Spracklen, K. (2001), 'Black Pearler, Black Diamond: Exploring Racial Identities in Rugby League', in B. Carrington and I. McDonald (eds), *Race, Sport and British Society*. London: Routledge.

Staurowsky, E. (2004), 'Piercing the Veil of Amateurism', in T. Slack (ed.), *The Commercialization of Sport*. London: Routledge.

Struna, N. (1997), 'Gender and Sporting Practice in Early America, 1750–1810', in D. Wiggins (ed.), *Sport in America*. Champaign, IL: Human Kinetics.

Thompson, J. (1986), 'Editor's Introduction', in C. Lefort (ed.), *The Political Forms of Modern Society*. Cambridge: MIT Press.

Tomlinson, A. (2004), 'The Disneyfication of the Olympics? Theme Parks and Freak-Shows of the Body', in J. Bale and M. Christensen (eds), *Post-Olympism?* Oxford: Berg.

— (ed.) (2007), *The Sports Studies Reader*. London: Routledge.

Tranter, N. (1998), *Sport, Economy and Society in Britain 1750–1914*. Cambridge: Cambridge University Press.

Vernant, J.-P. and Vidal-Naquet, P. (1990), *Myth and Tragedy in Ancient Greece*, trans. J. Lloyd. New York: Zone Books.

Vertinsky, P. and Bale, J. (eds) (2004), *Sites of Sport*. London: Routledge.

Vincent, T. (1994), *The Rise and Fall of American Sport*. Lincoln: University of Nebraska Press.

Wagg, S. (ed.) (2005), *Cricket and National Identity in the Postcolonial Age*. London: Routledge.

Waugh, T. (1910), *The Cricket Field of a Christian Life*. Stockport: n.p.

Whannel, G. (2002), *Media Sports Stars*. London: Routledge.

— (2007), 'Mediating Masculinities', in C. Aitchison (ed.), *Sport and Gendered Identities*. London: Routledge.

— (2009), 'Understanding the Politics of Media Sport', in B. Carrington and
   I. McDonald (eds), *Marxism, Cultural Studies and Sport*. London: Routledge.
Wiggins, D. (ed.) (1997), *Sport in America*. Champaign, IL: Human Kinetics.
Williams, J. (2001), *Cricket and Race*. Oxford: Berg.
Wittgenstein, L. (1983), *Philosophical Investigations*. Oxford: Blackwell.
Woodward, D. (2004), 'A Whole New Ballgame: How Fantasy Sport Has Evolved
   in the Mass Media', Dissertation for Master of Arts in Communication
   University of Texas Arlington http://dspace.uta.edu/handle/10106/340
Woodward, K. (2007), *Boxing, Masculinity and Identity*. London: Routledge.
Zillgitt, J. (2000), 'We Certainly Live in a Fantasy World', USAToday.com www.
   usatoday.com/sports/comment/jzcol53.htm
Zizek, S. (1991), *For They Know Not What They Do*. London: Verso.
— (1992), *The Sublime Object of Ideology*. London: Verso.

INDEX